Flip It!
Colouring book

Sugar Skulls

By

Tim Gold

©2017 theqpress@yahoo.com

ISBN: 978-0-244-67521-9

Bring these beautiful creations to life in your own way by adding a splash of colour and your unique style. Simply colour in the images and then flip through the book to create your very own one of a kind flipbook.

There are two designs on either side of the page for you to play with and make your own.

We recommend using light pastel colours for your shading and colouring as not to interfere with the image on the reverse of the page

That's it really....... Get your pencils at the ready and go!

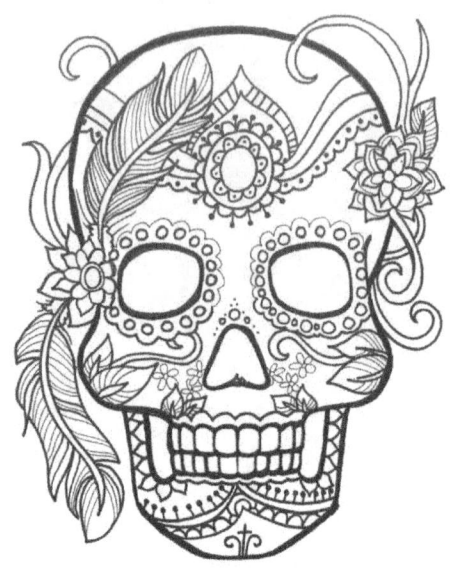
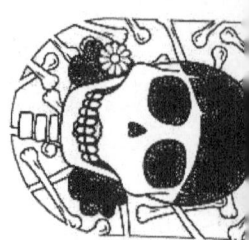
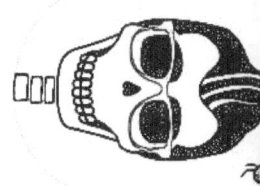
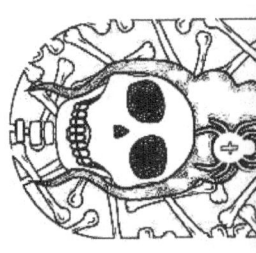
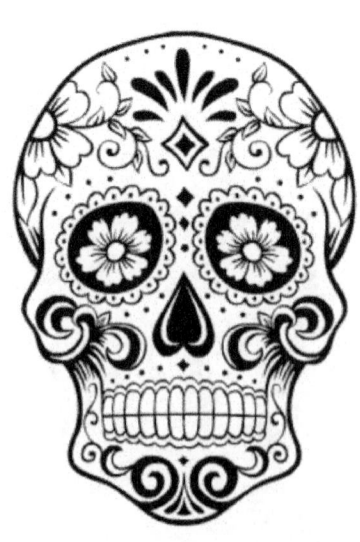
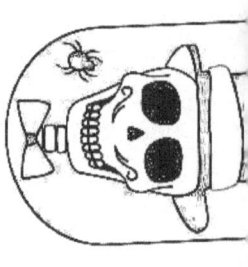

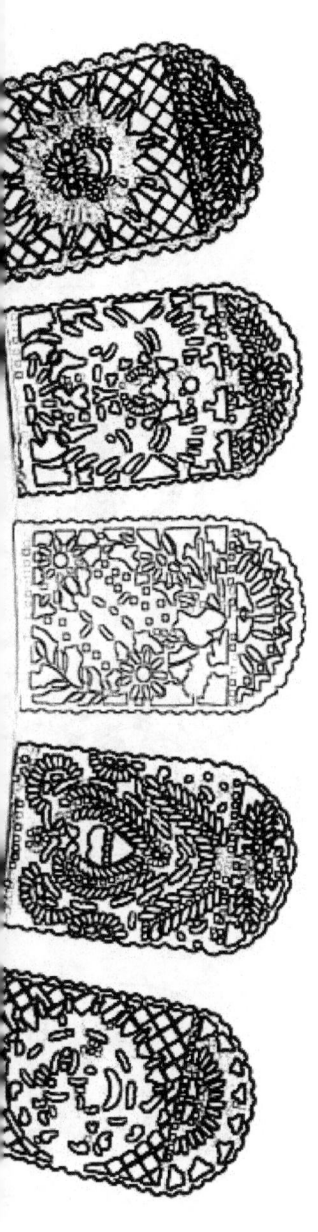
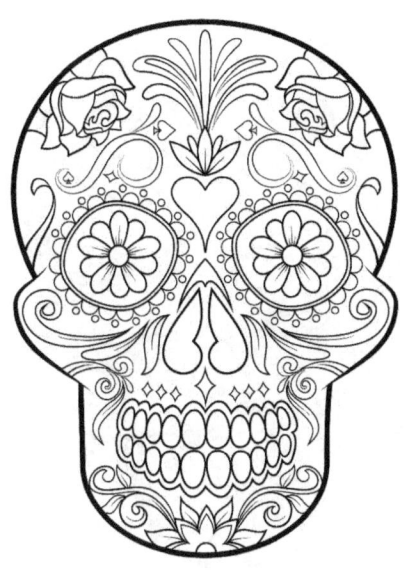
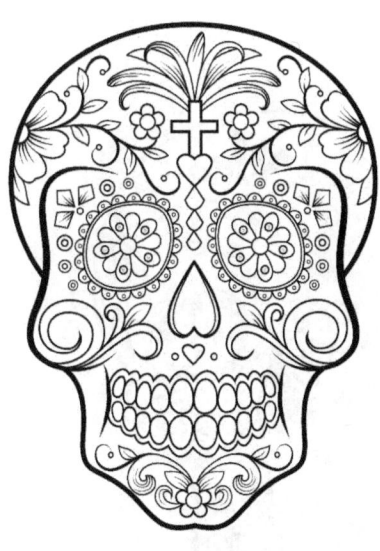

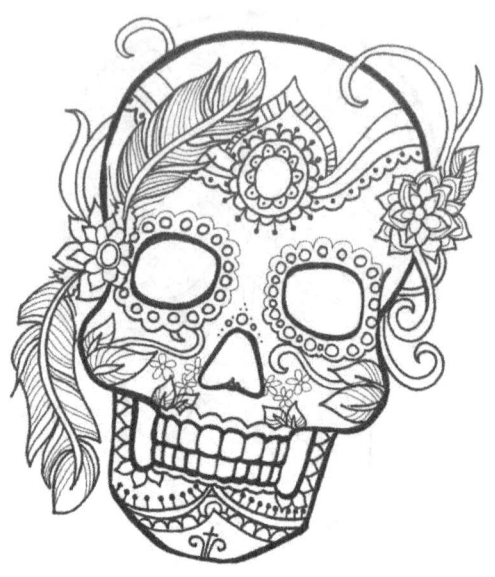

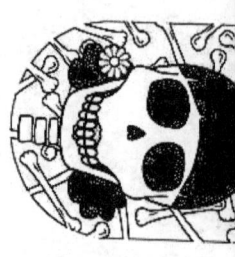

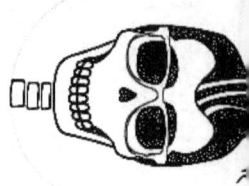

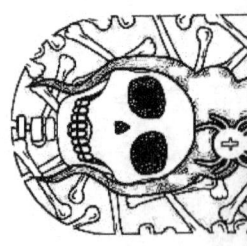

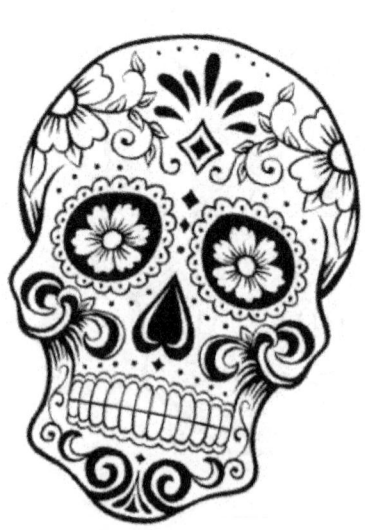

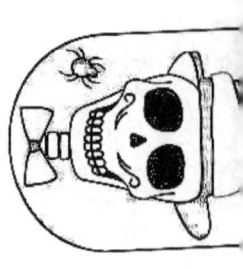

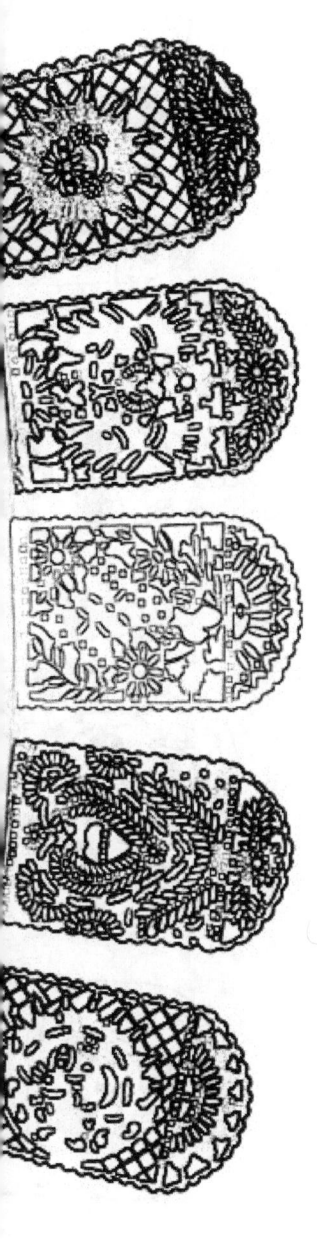

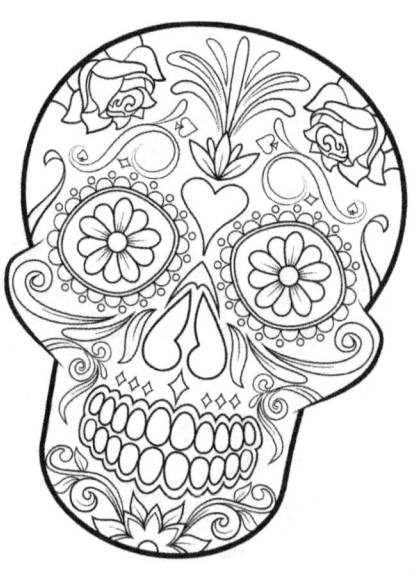

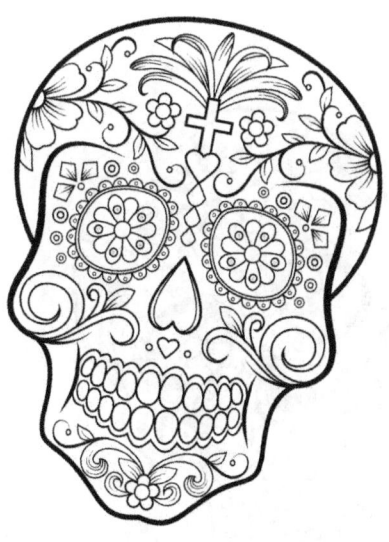

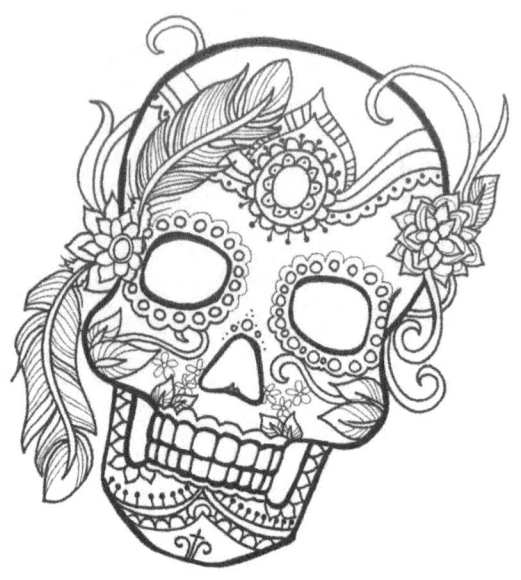
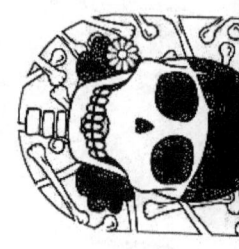
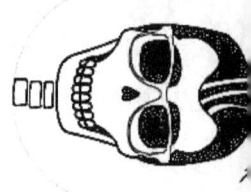
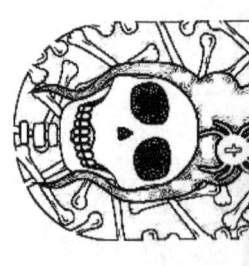
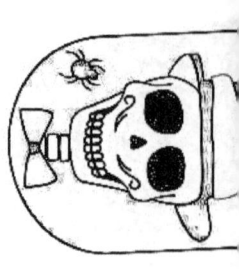
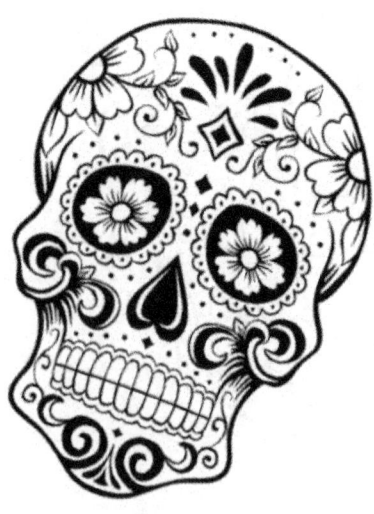

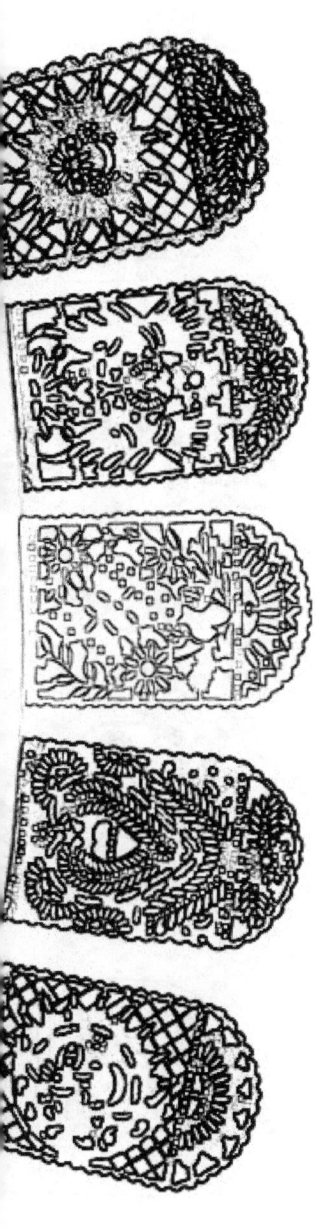
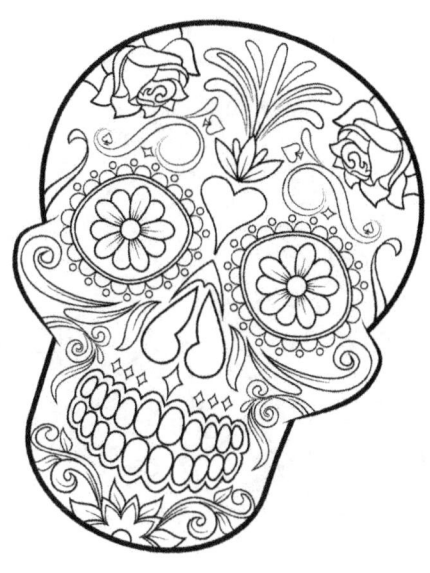
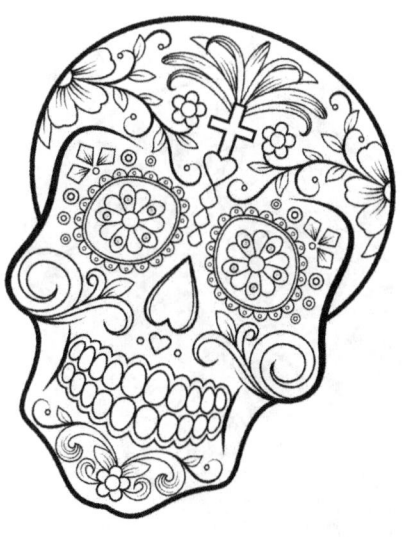

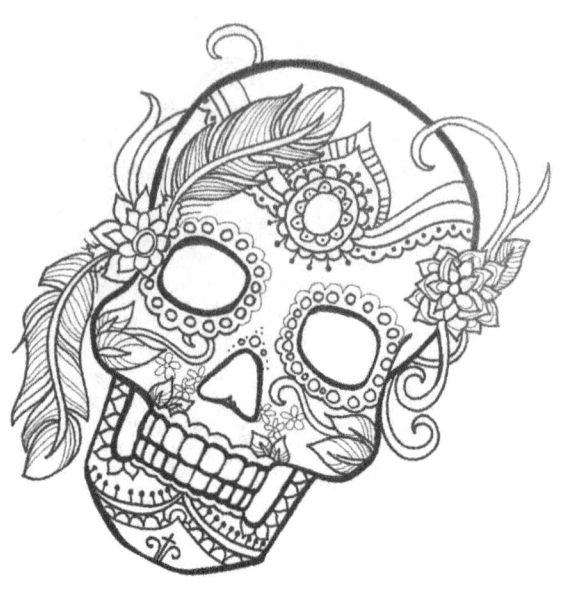
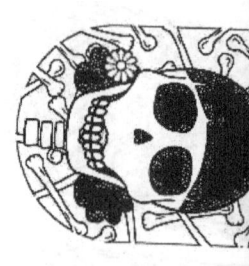
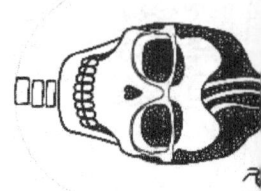
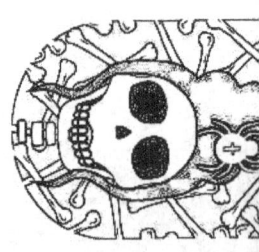
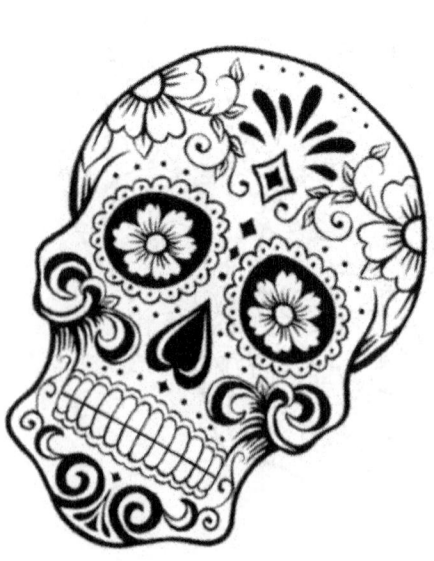
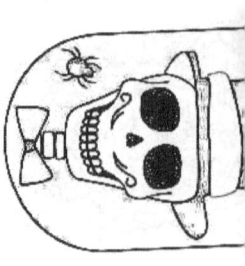

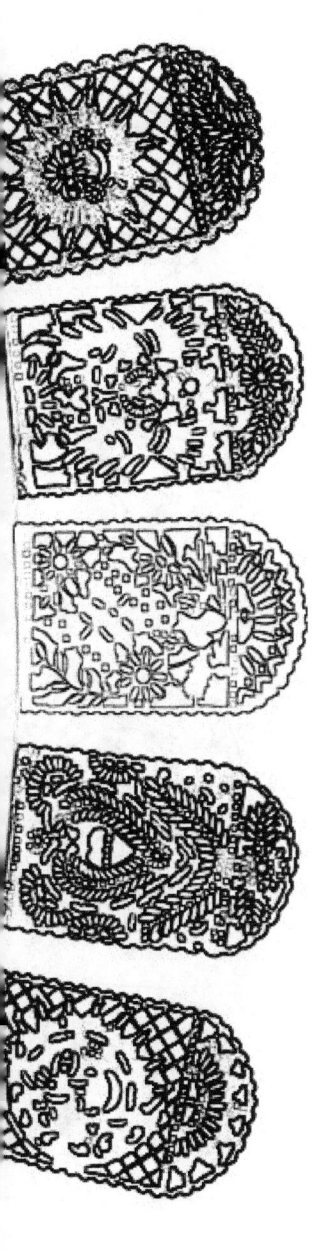

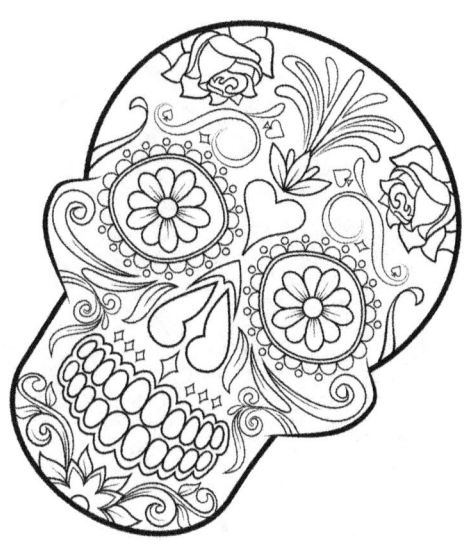

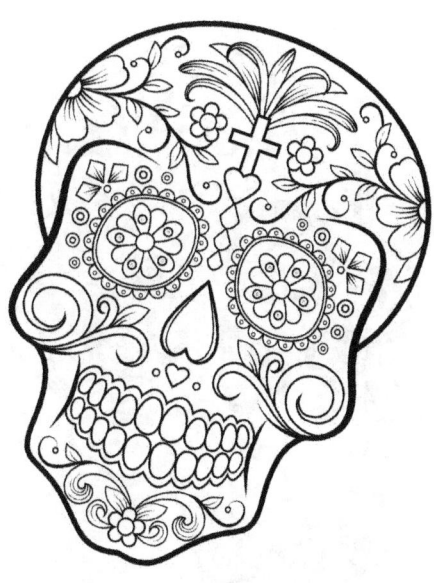

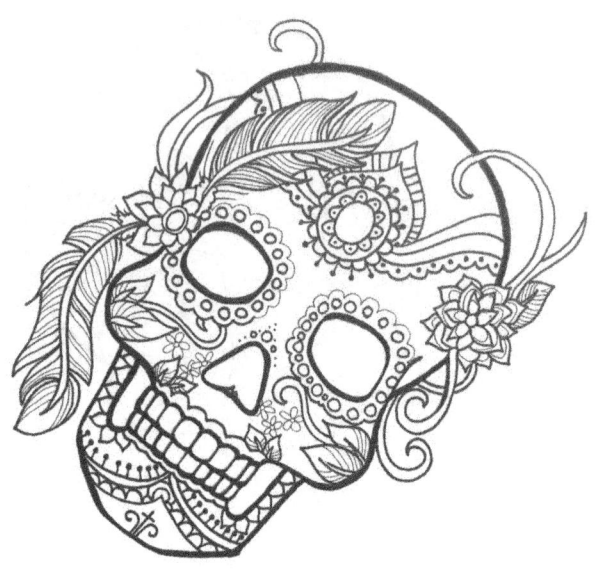
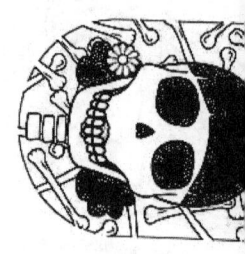
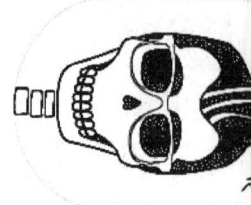
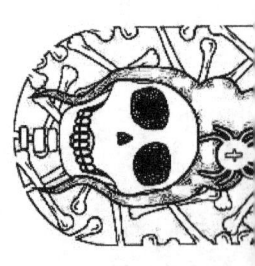
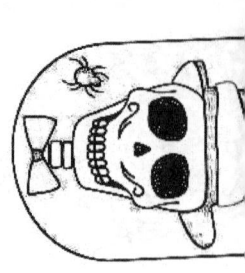
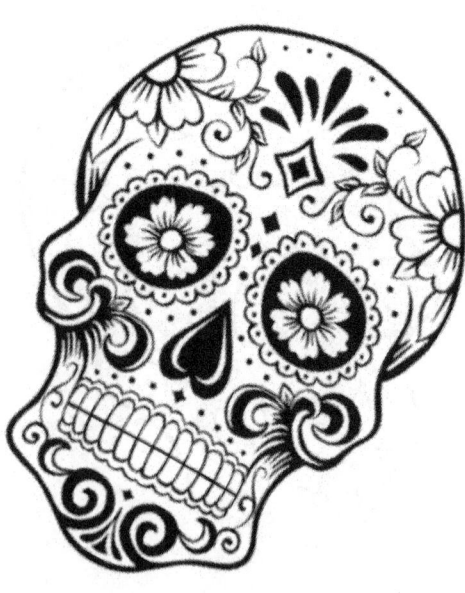

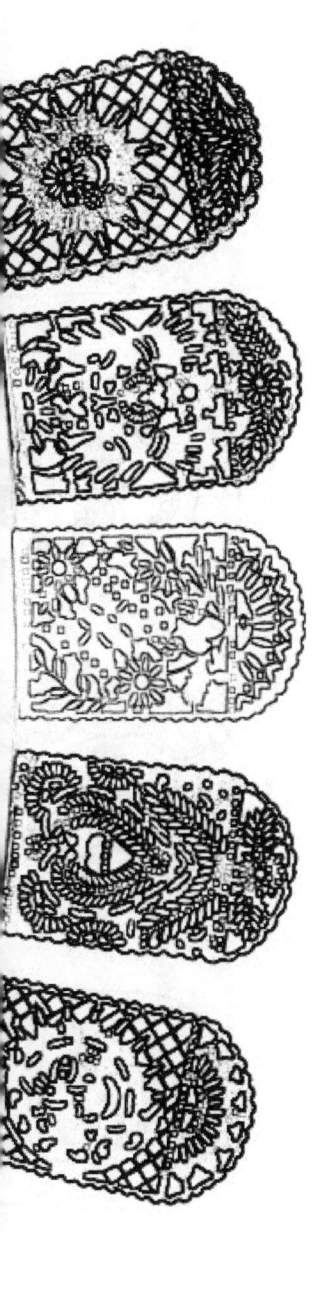
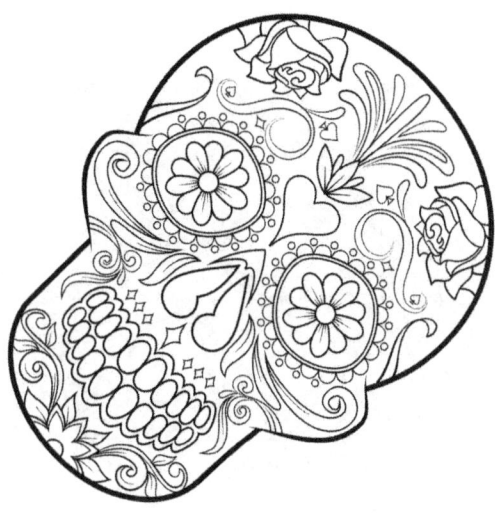
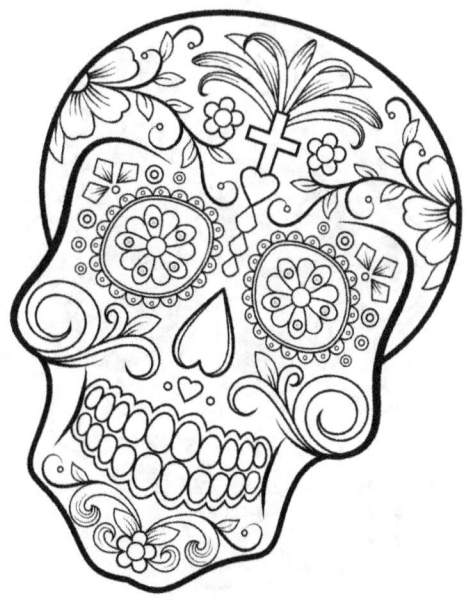

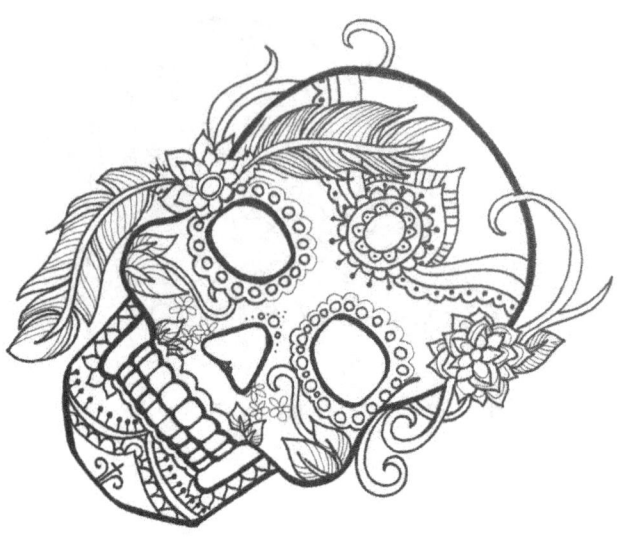
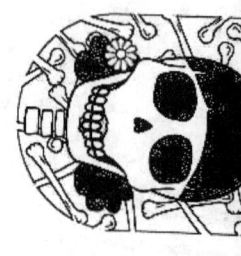
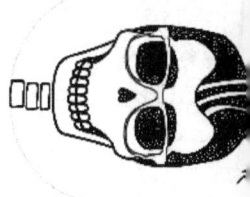
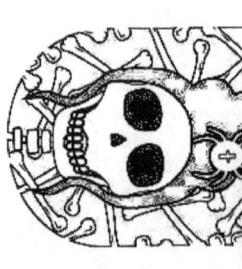
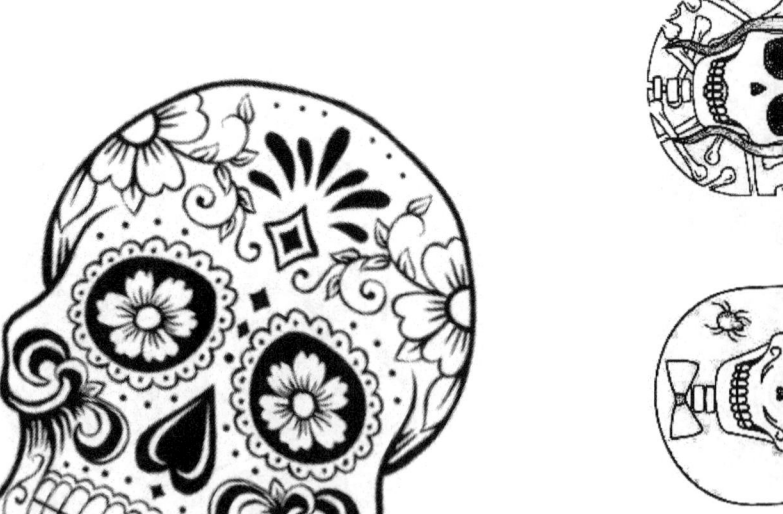
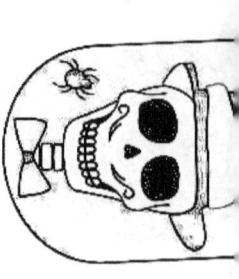

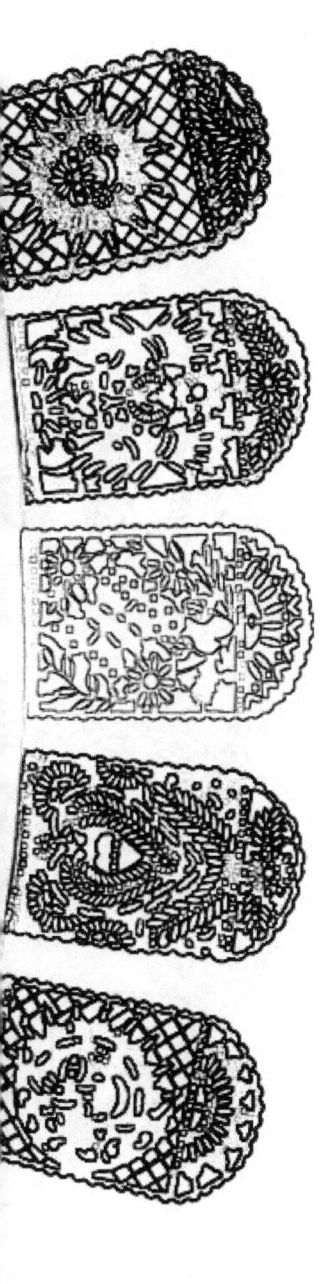
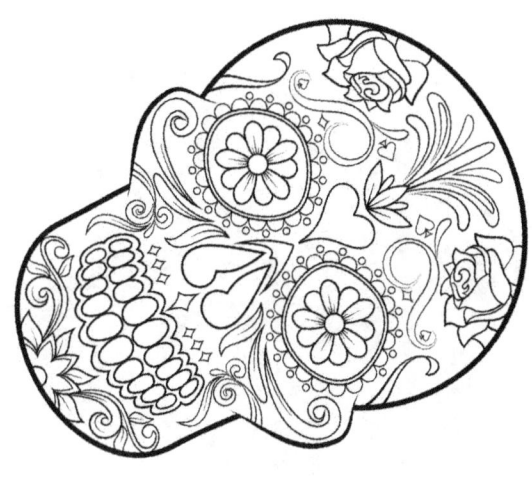
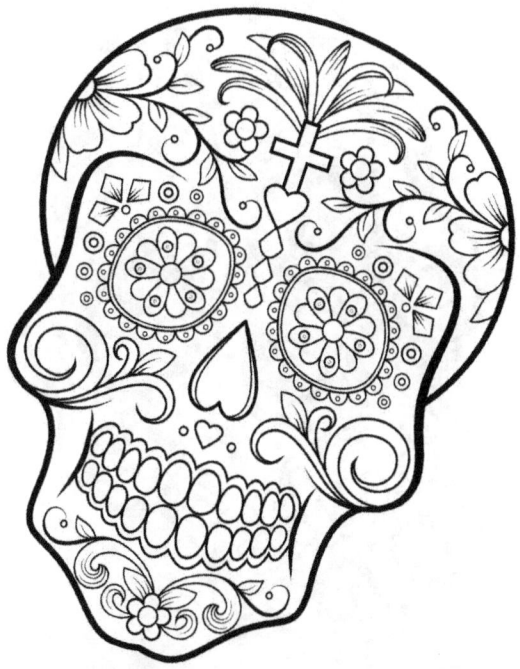

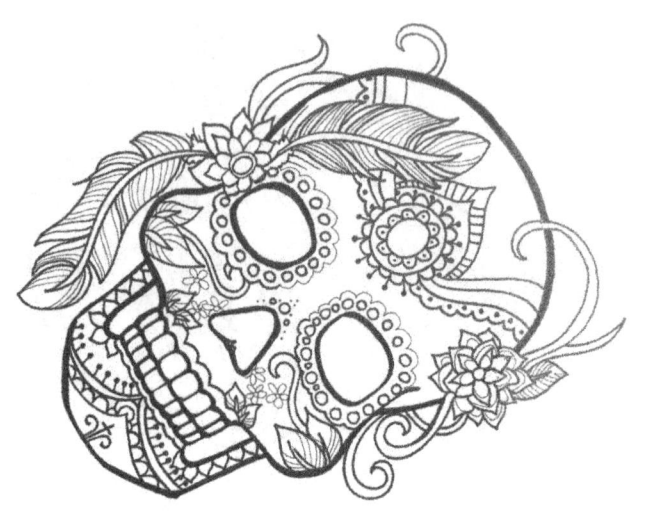
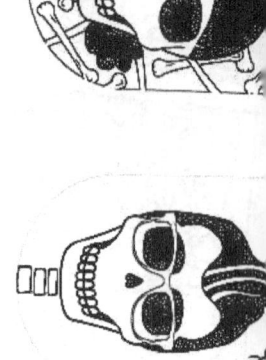
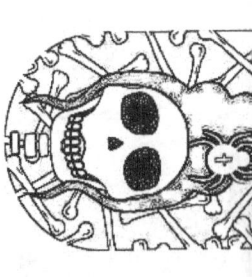
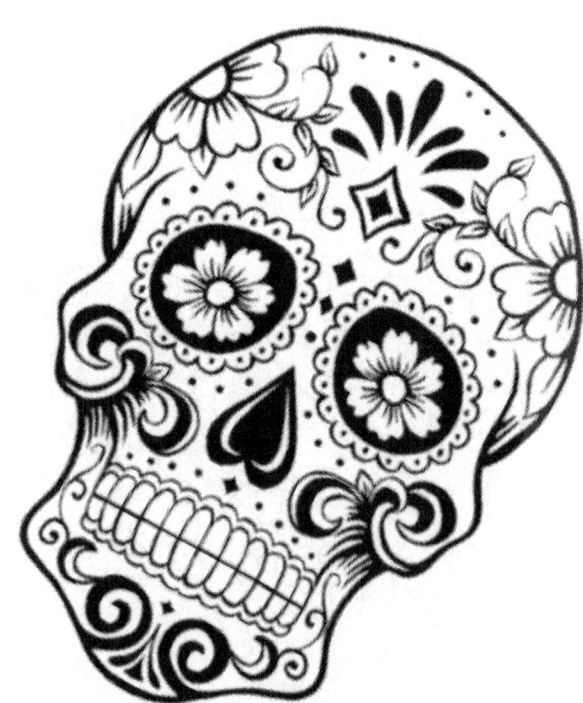
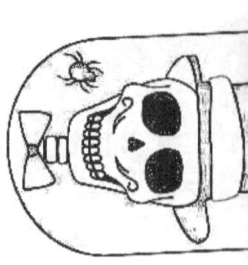

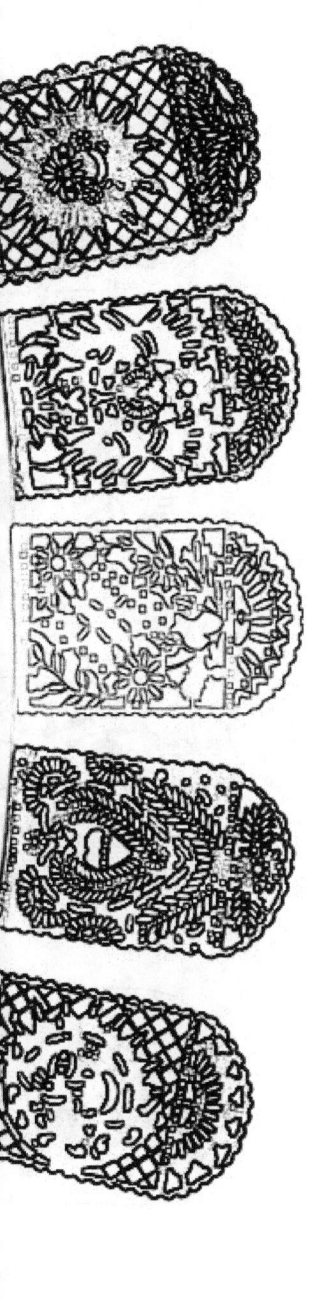
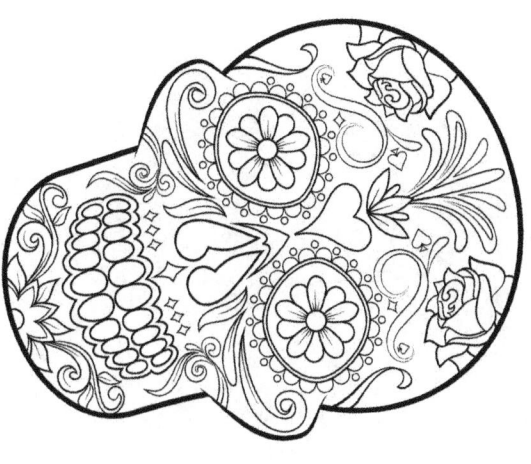
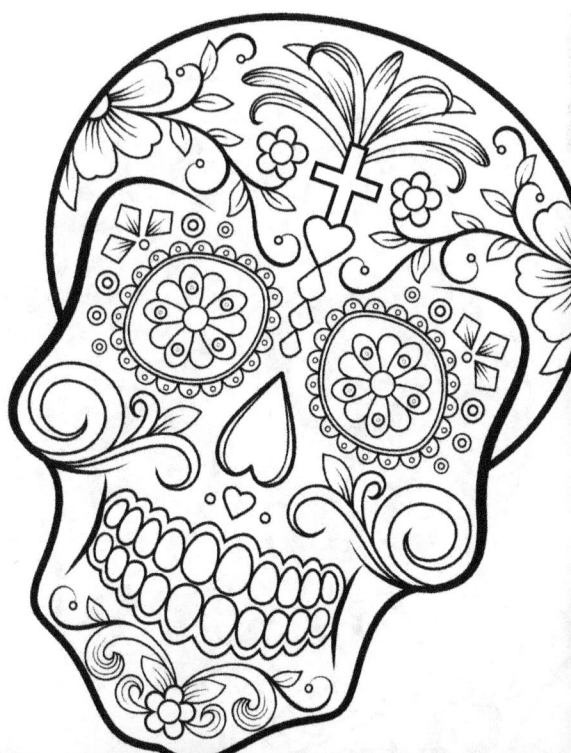

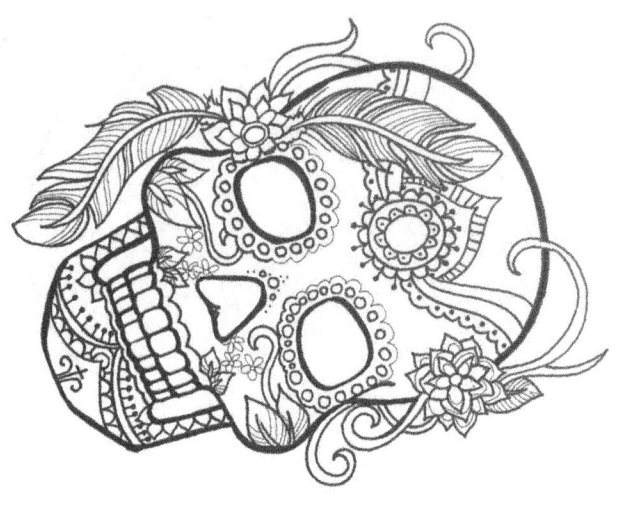
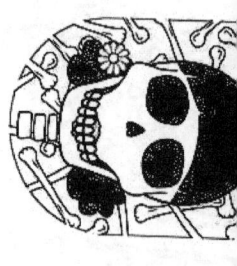
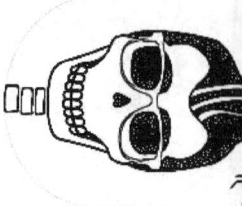
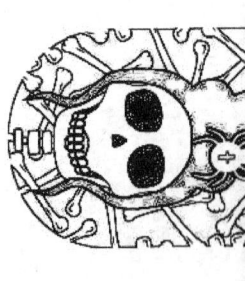
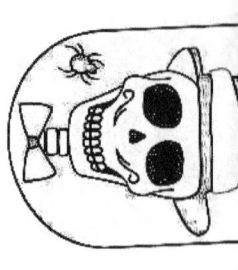
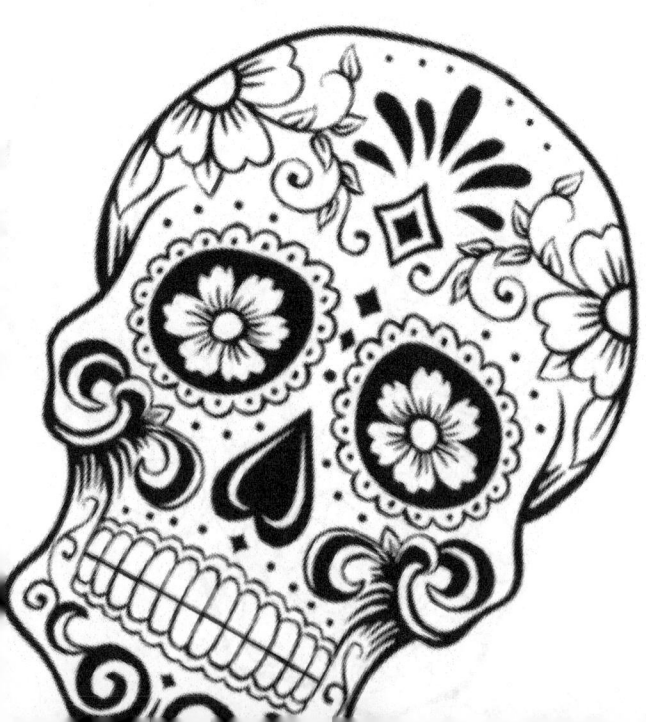

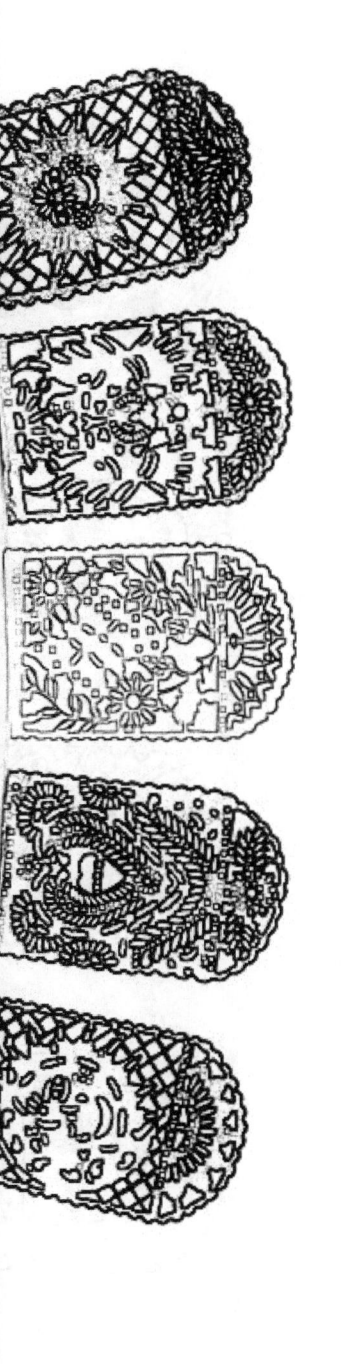
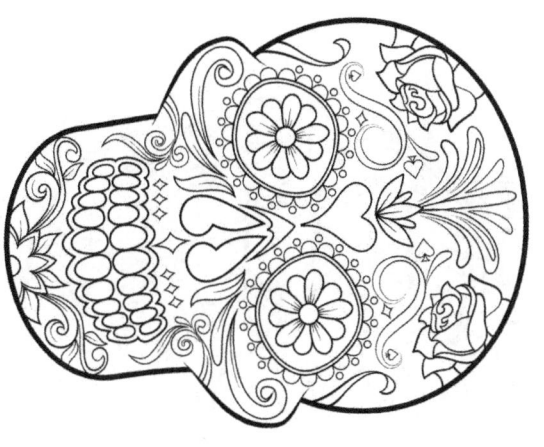
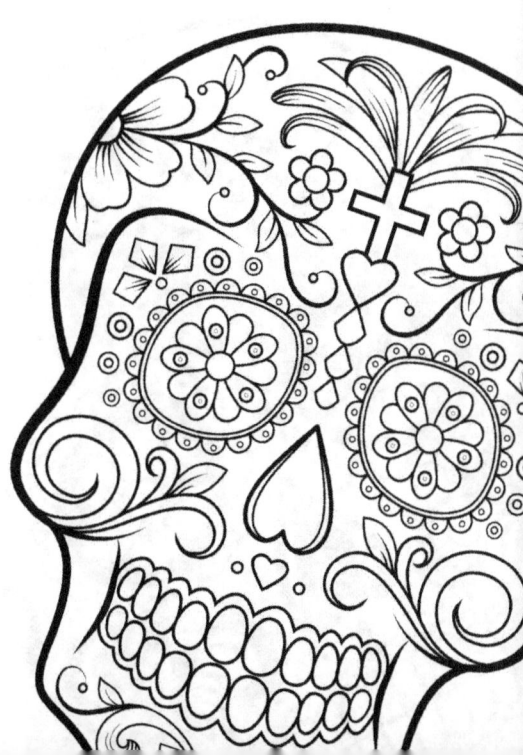

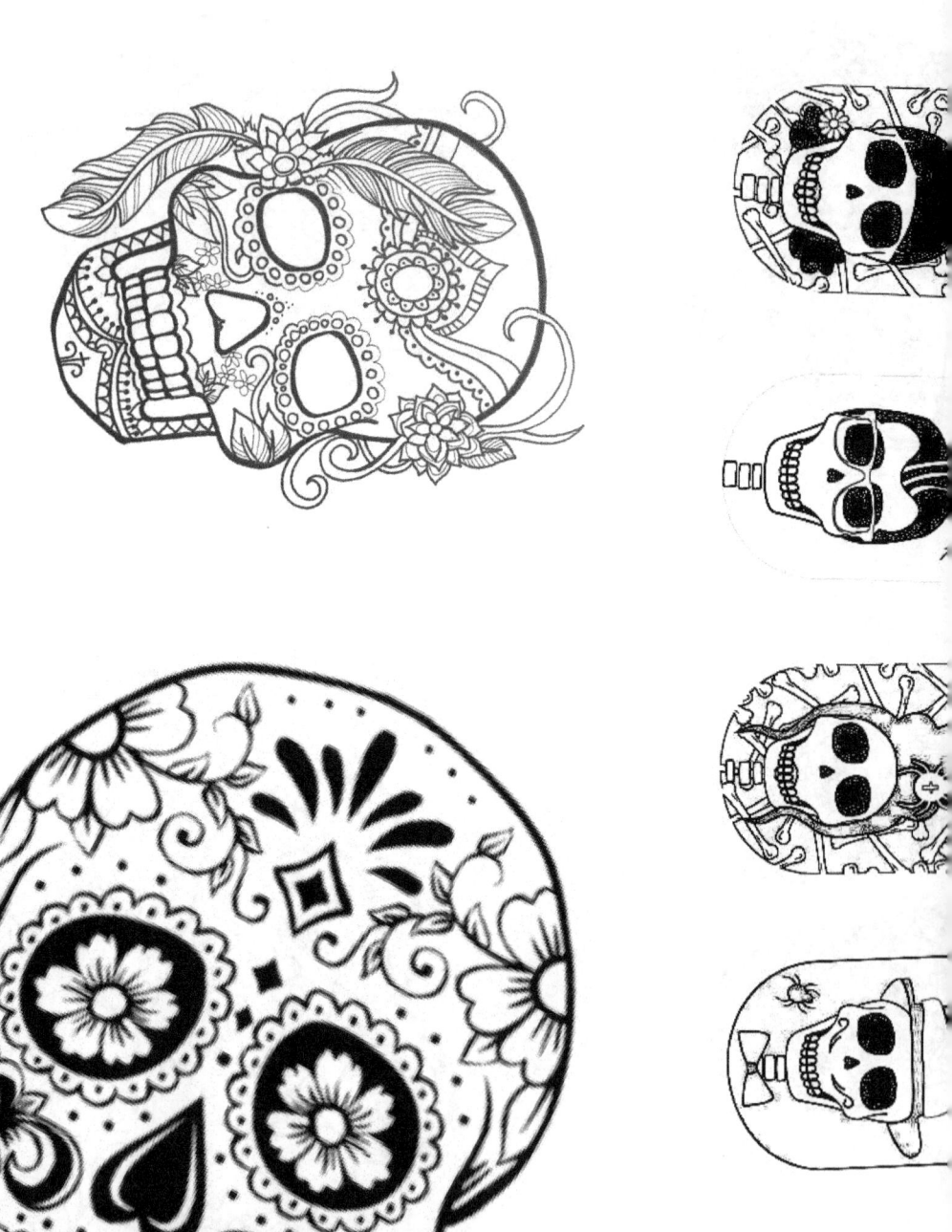

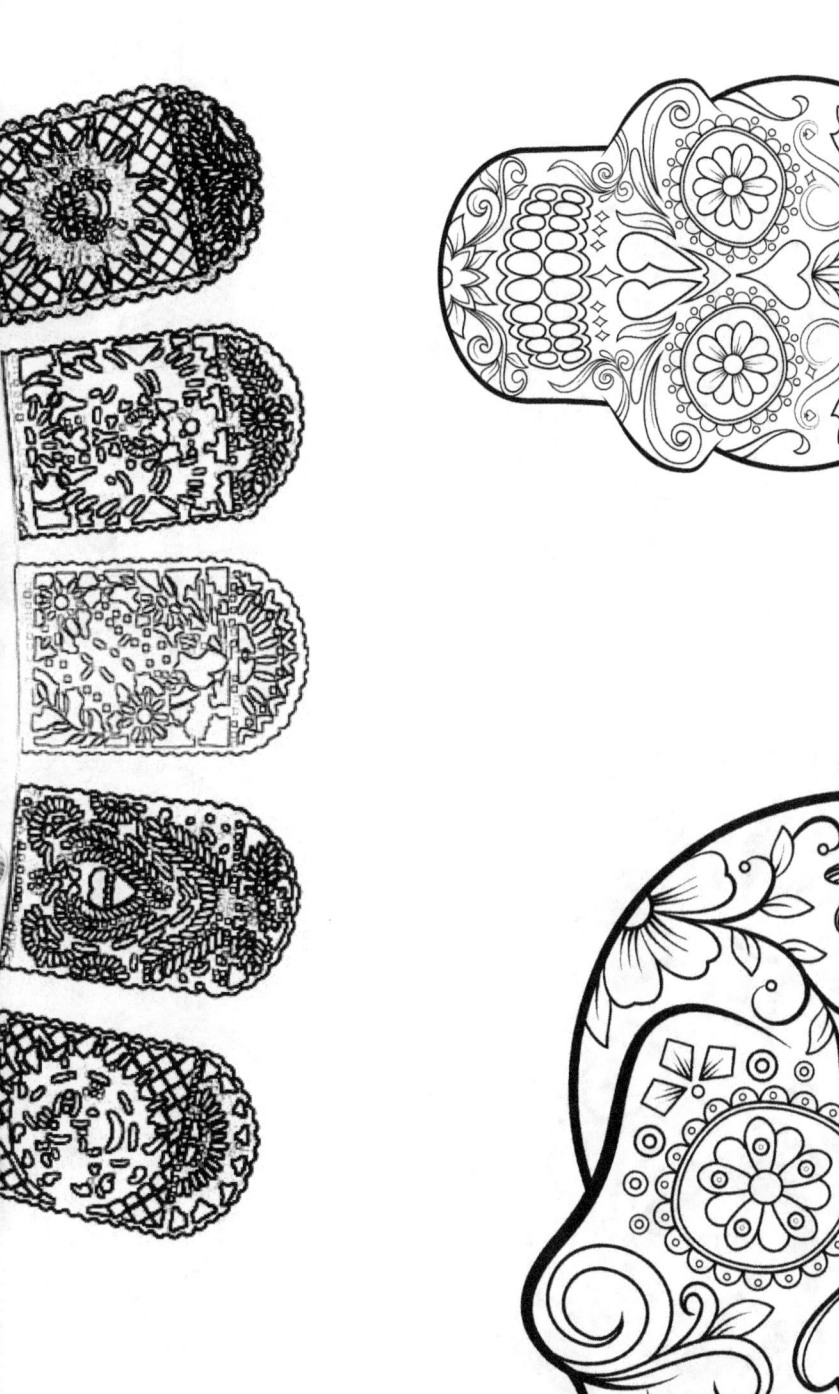

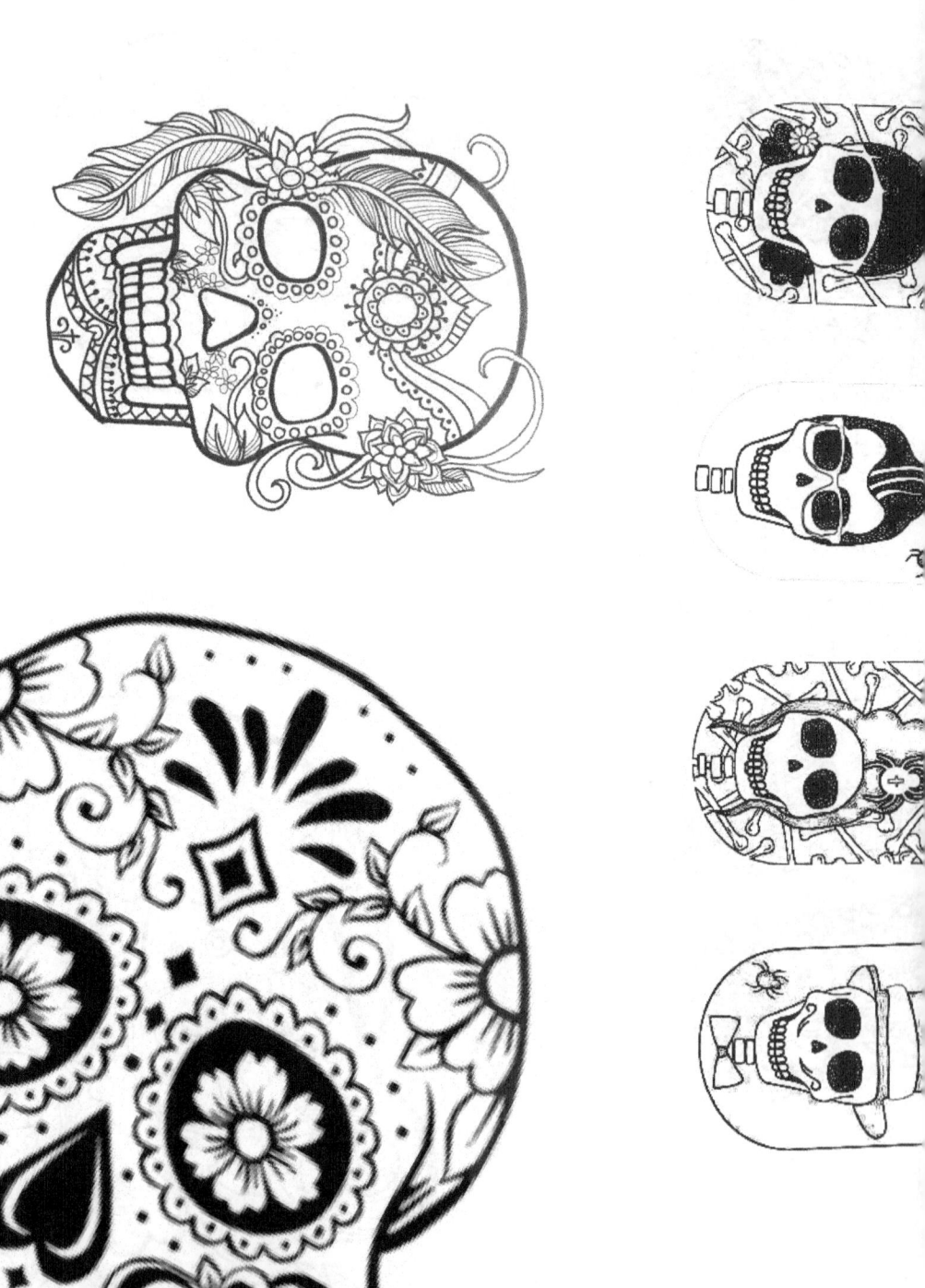

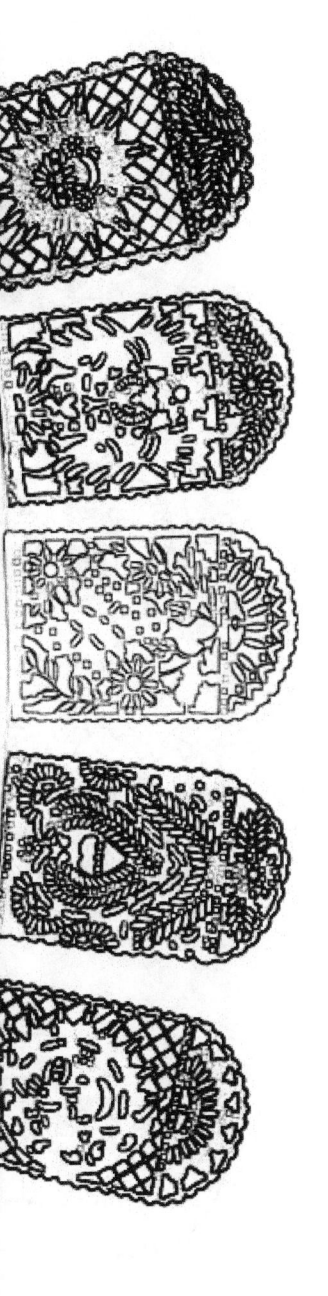
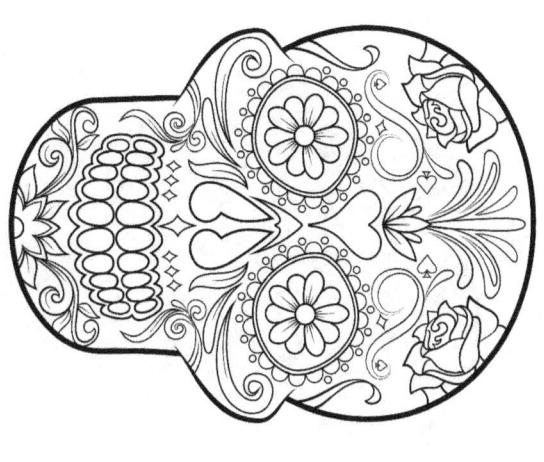
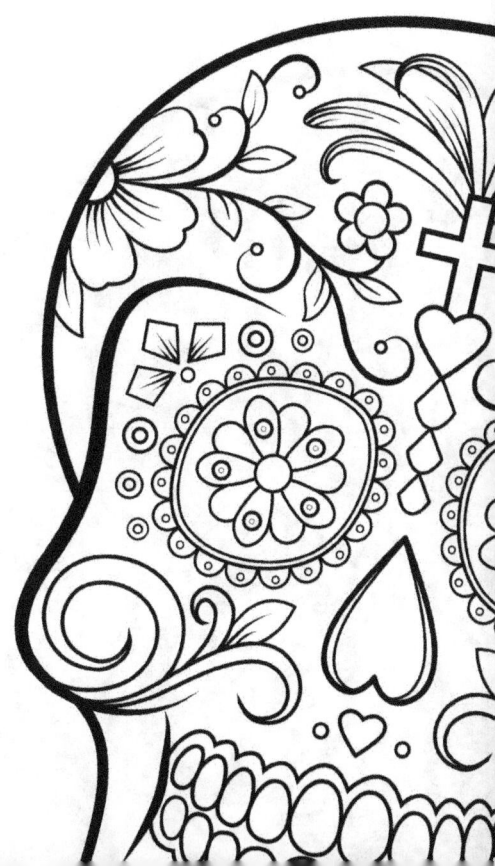

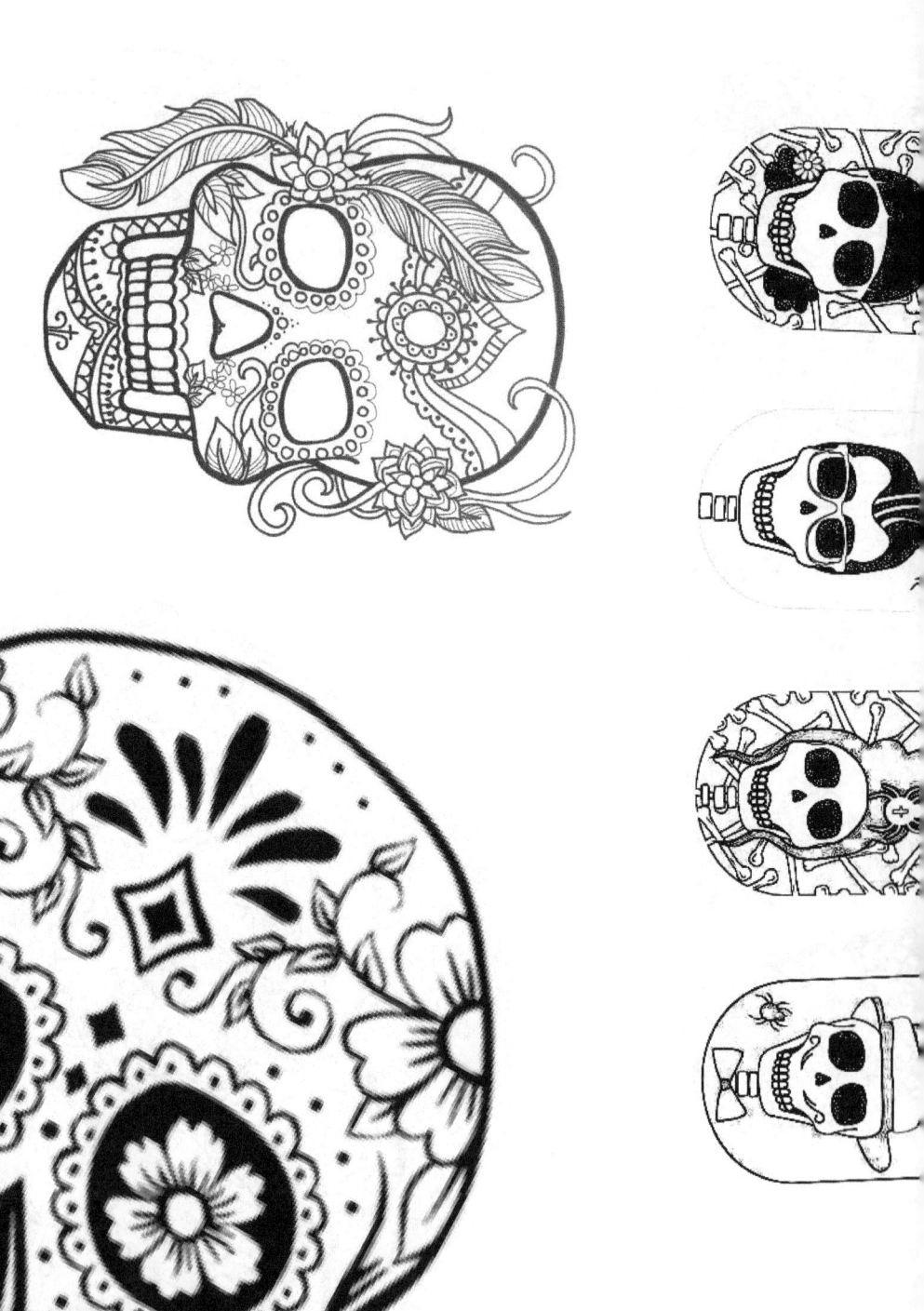

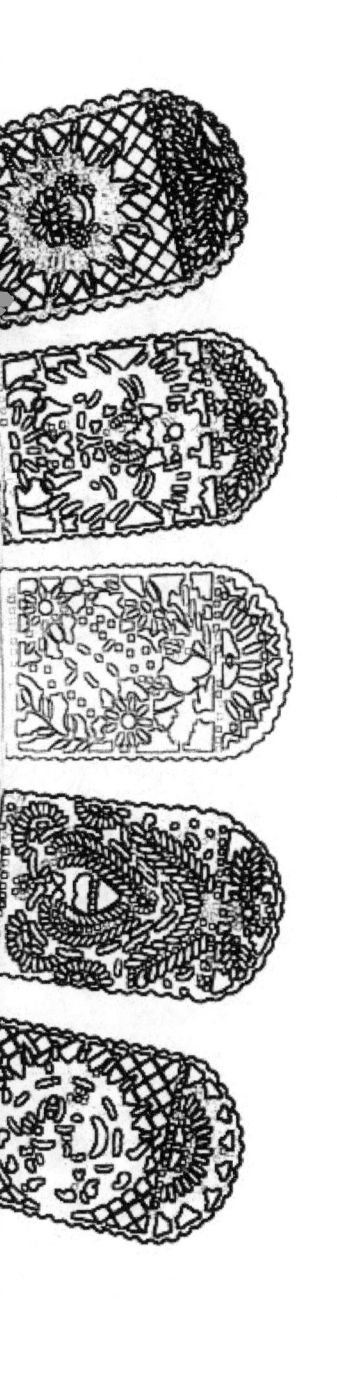
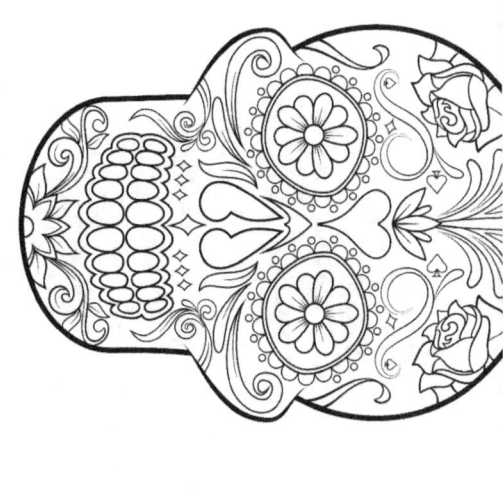
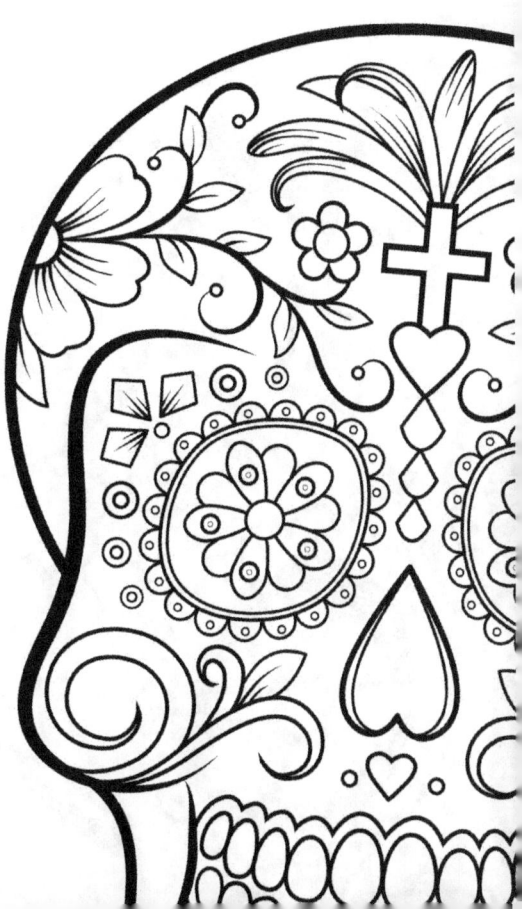

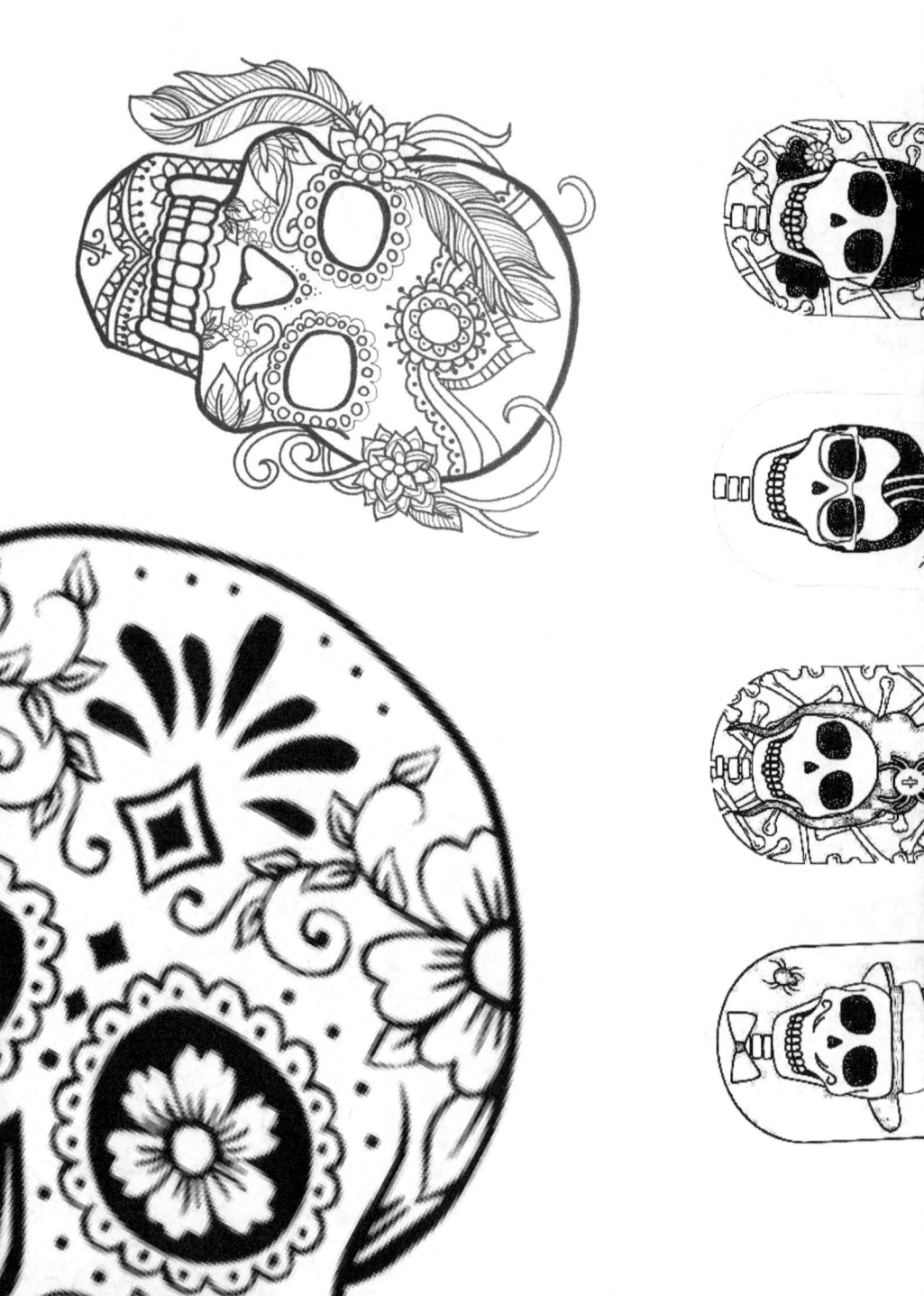

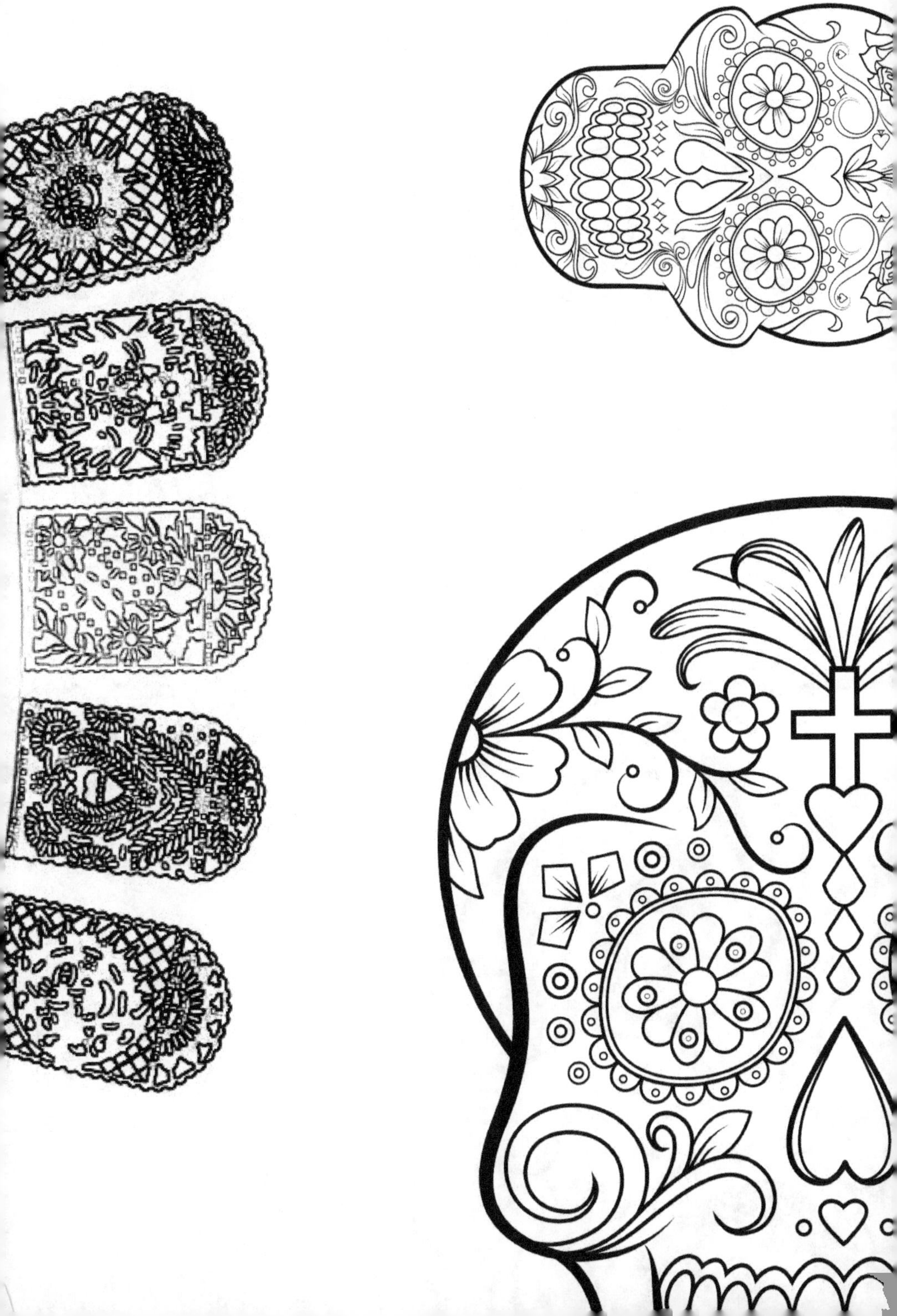

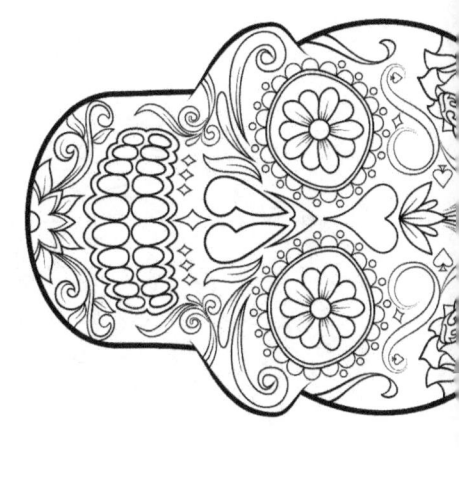

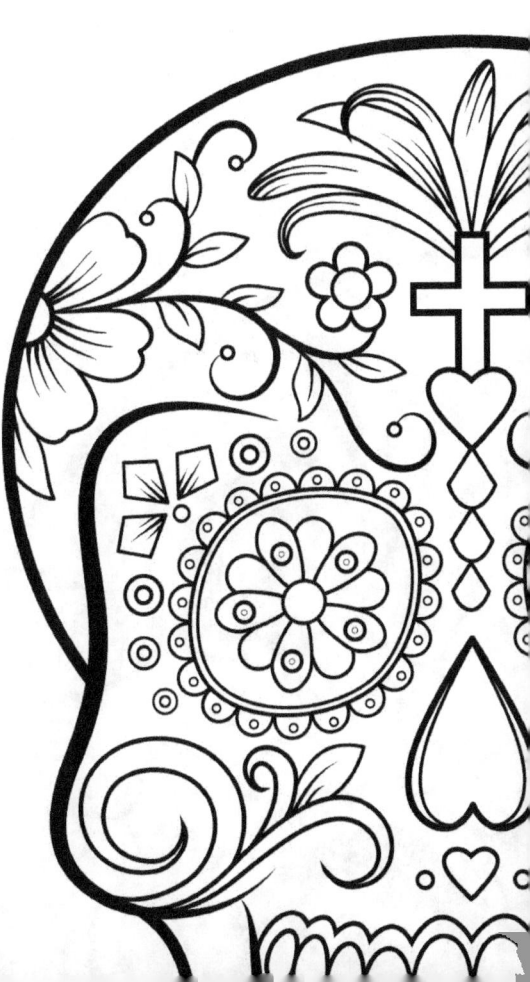

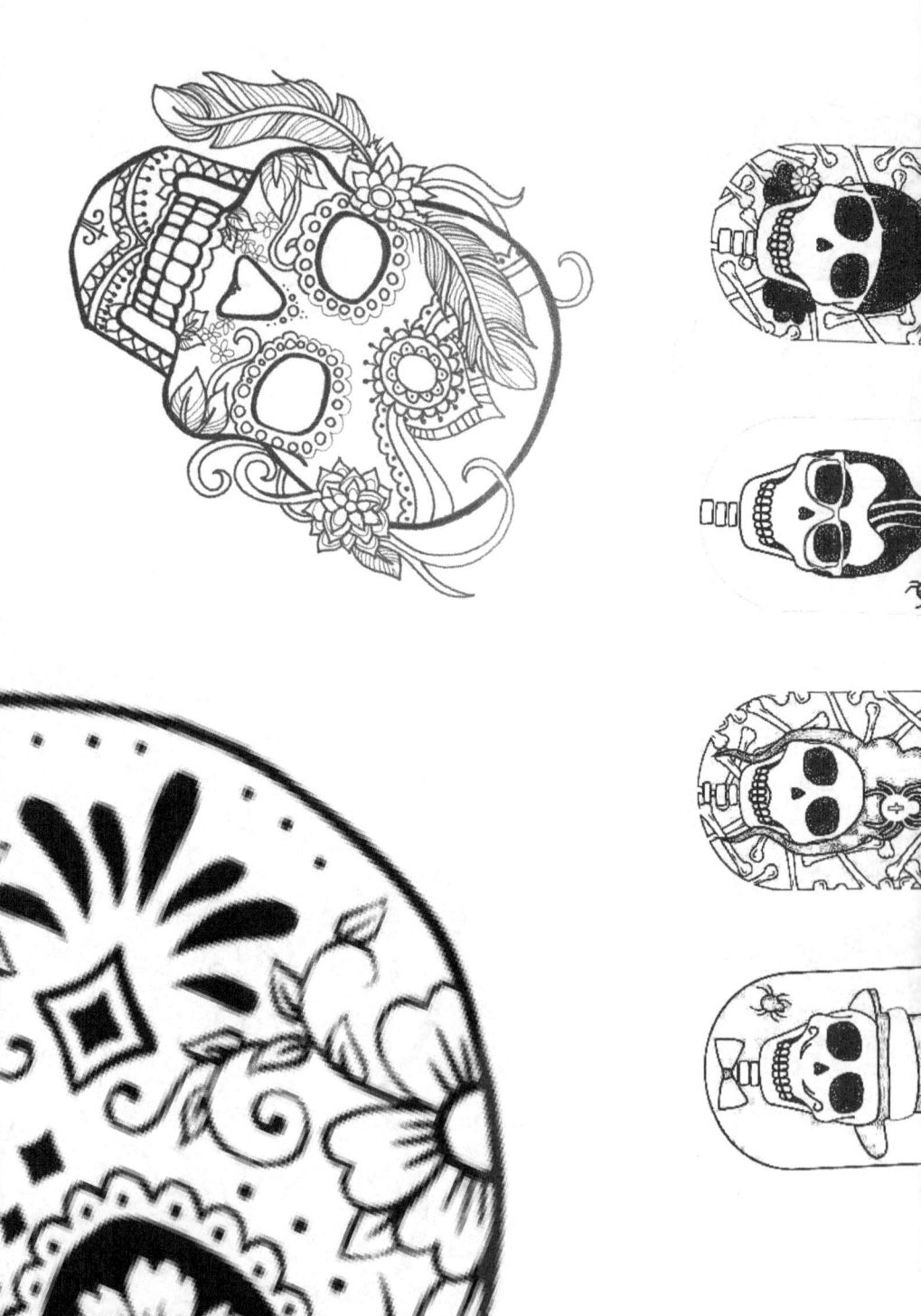

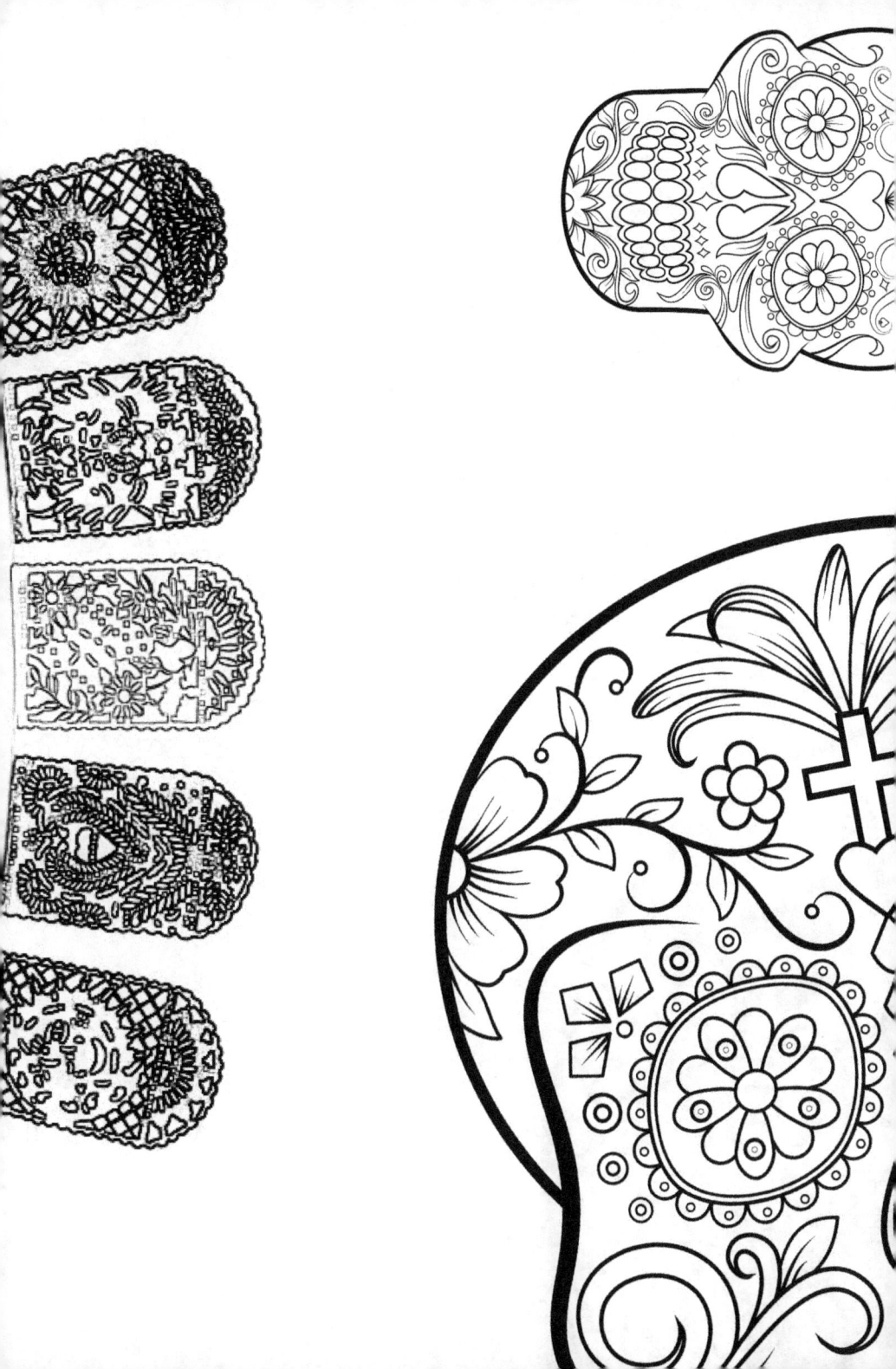

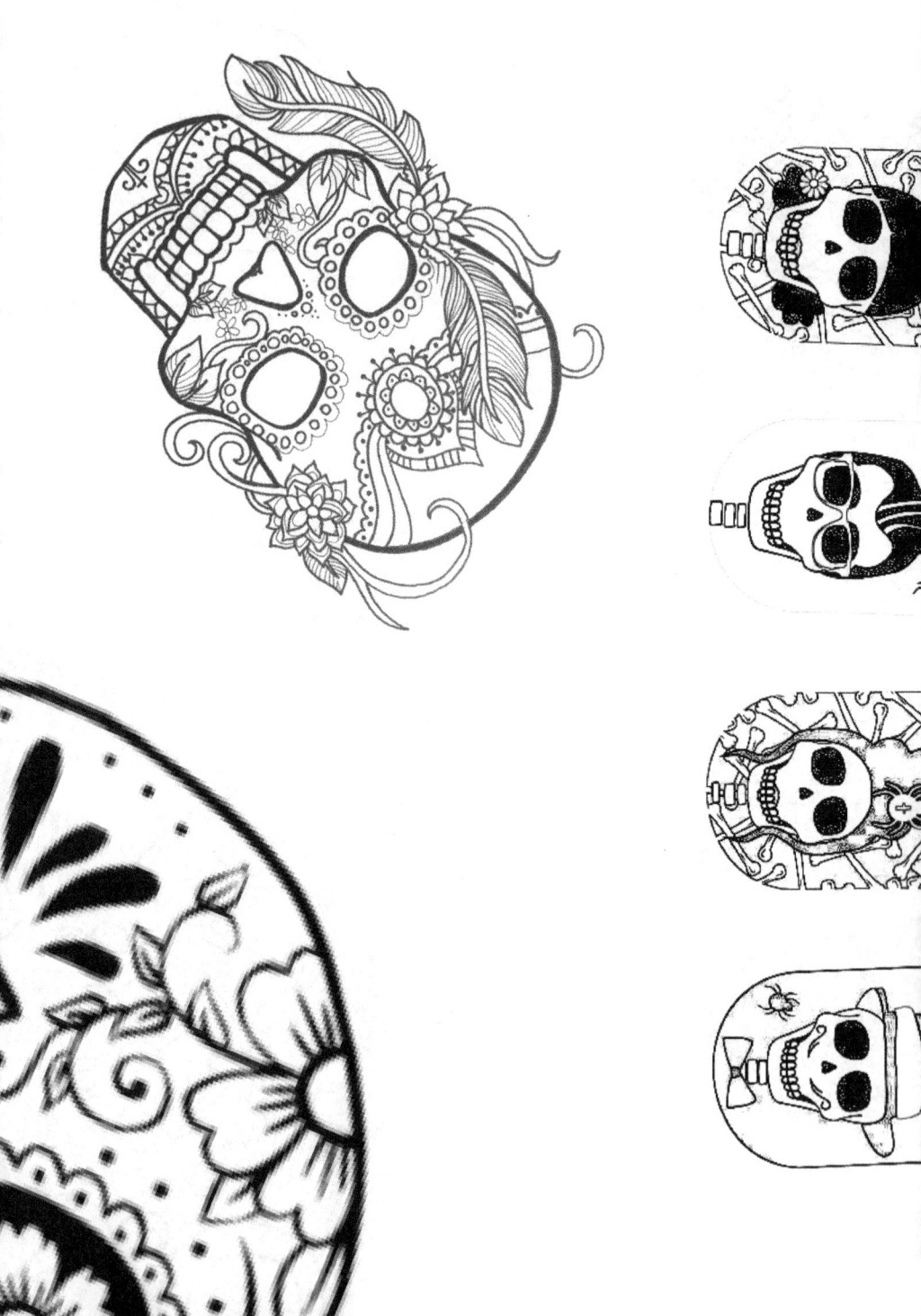

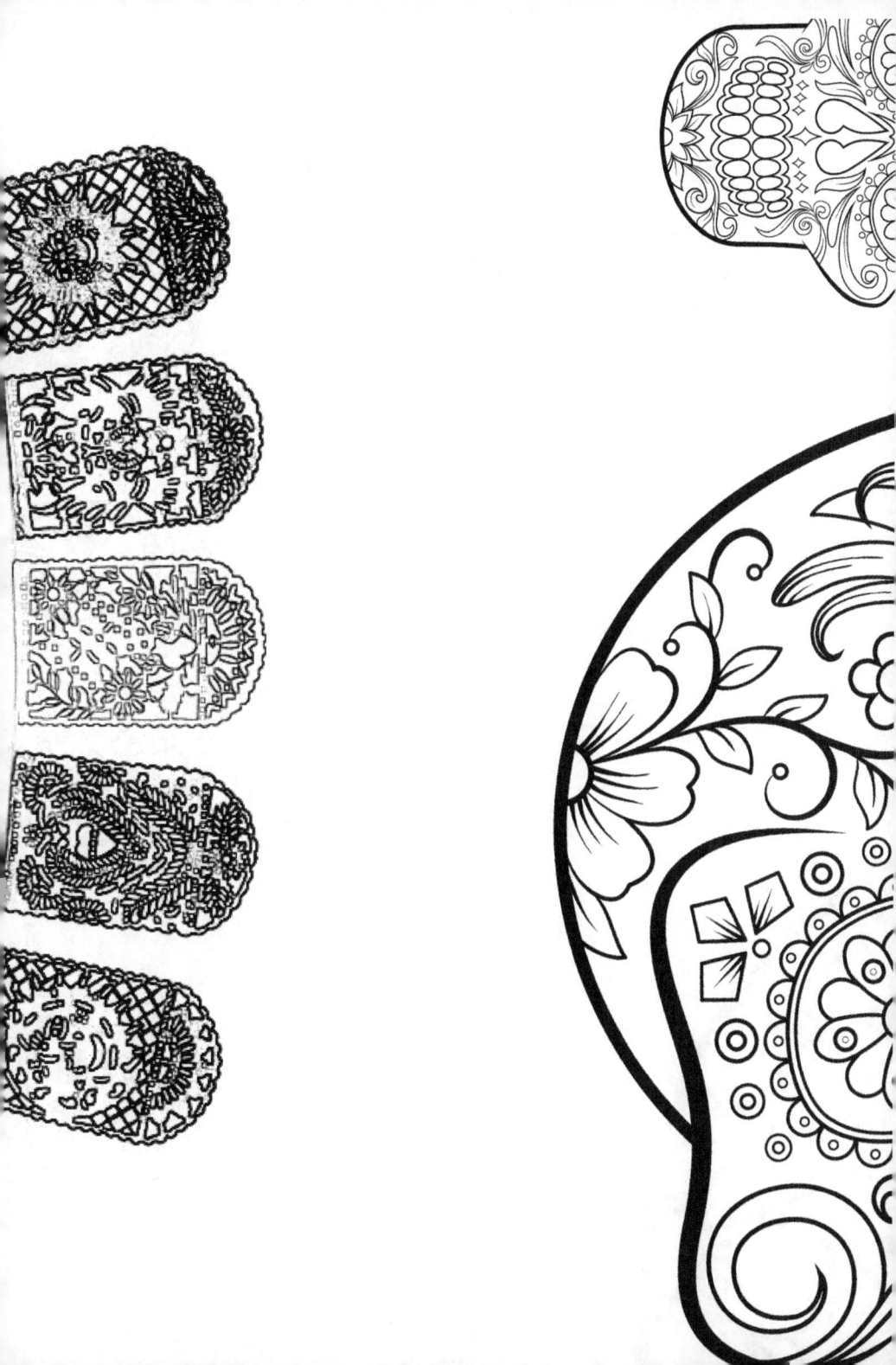

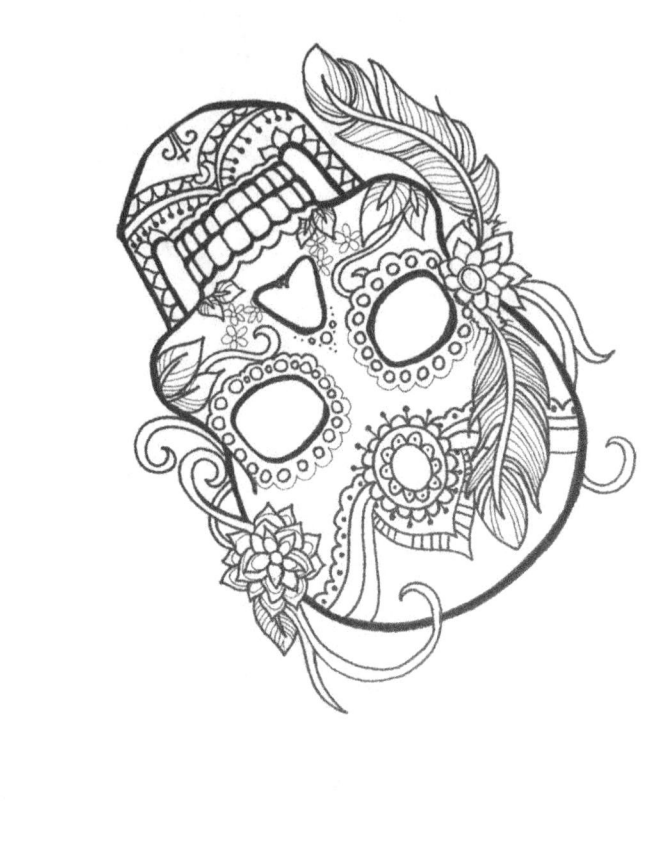
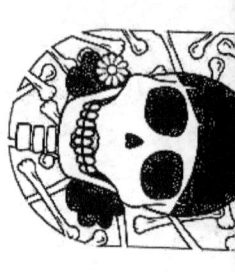
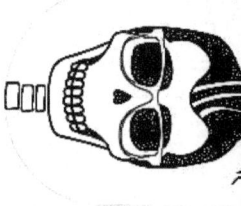
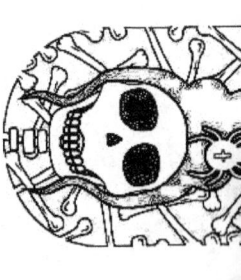
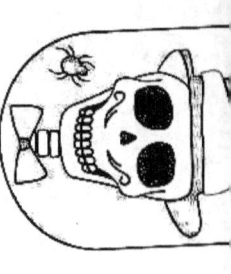
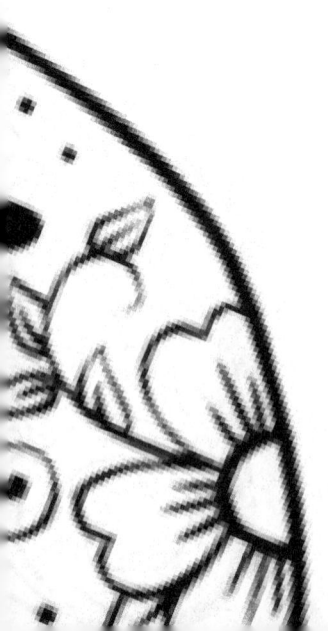

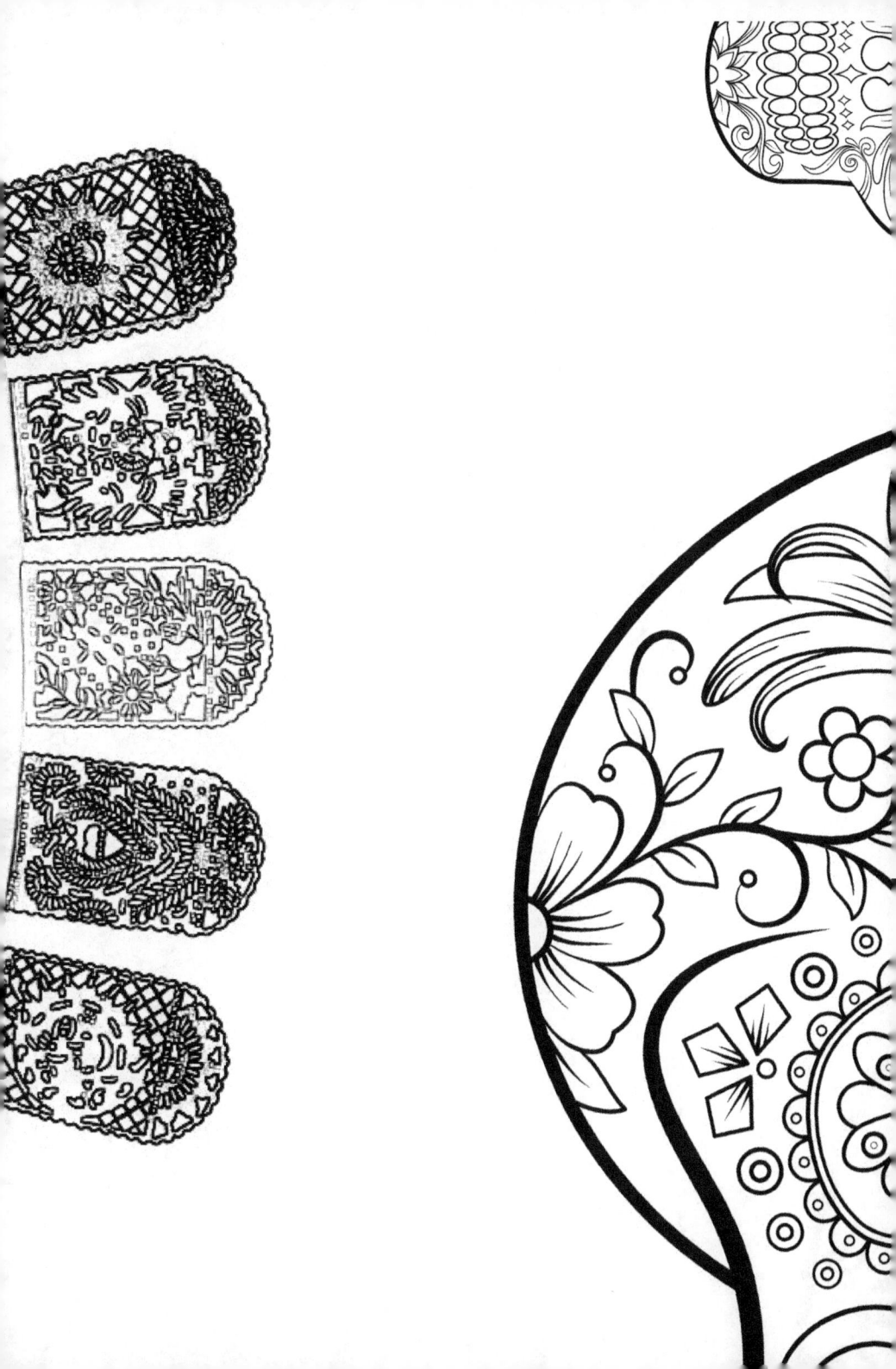

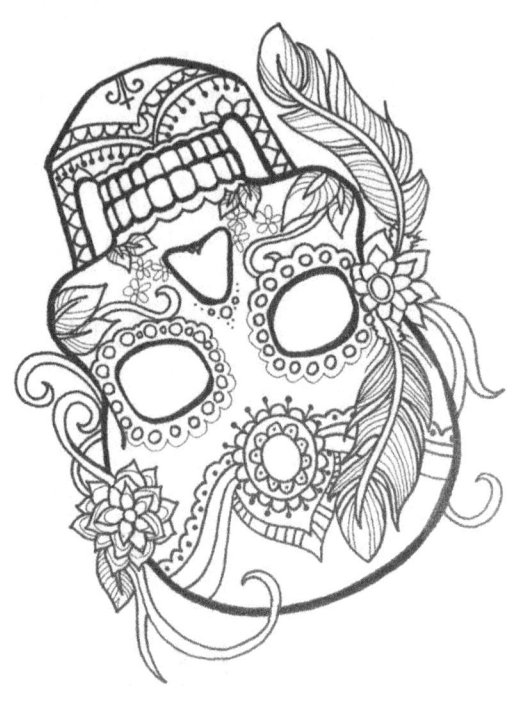

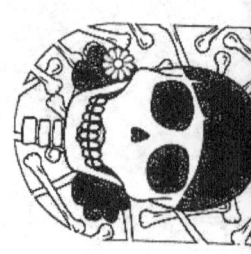

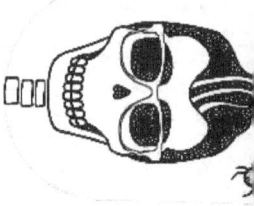

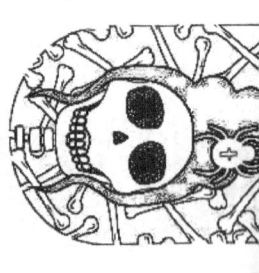

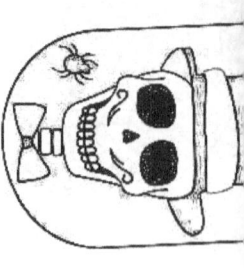

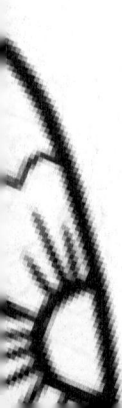

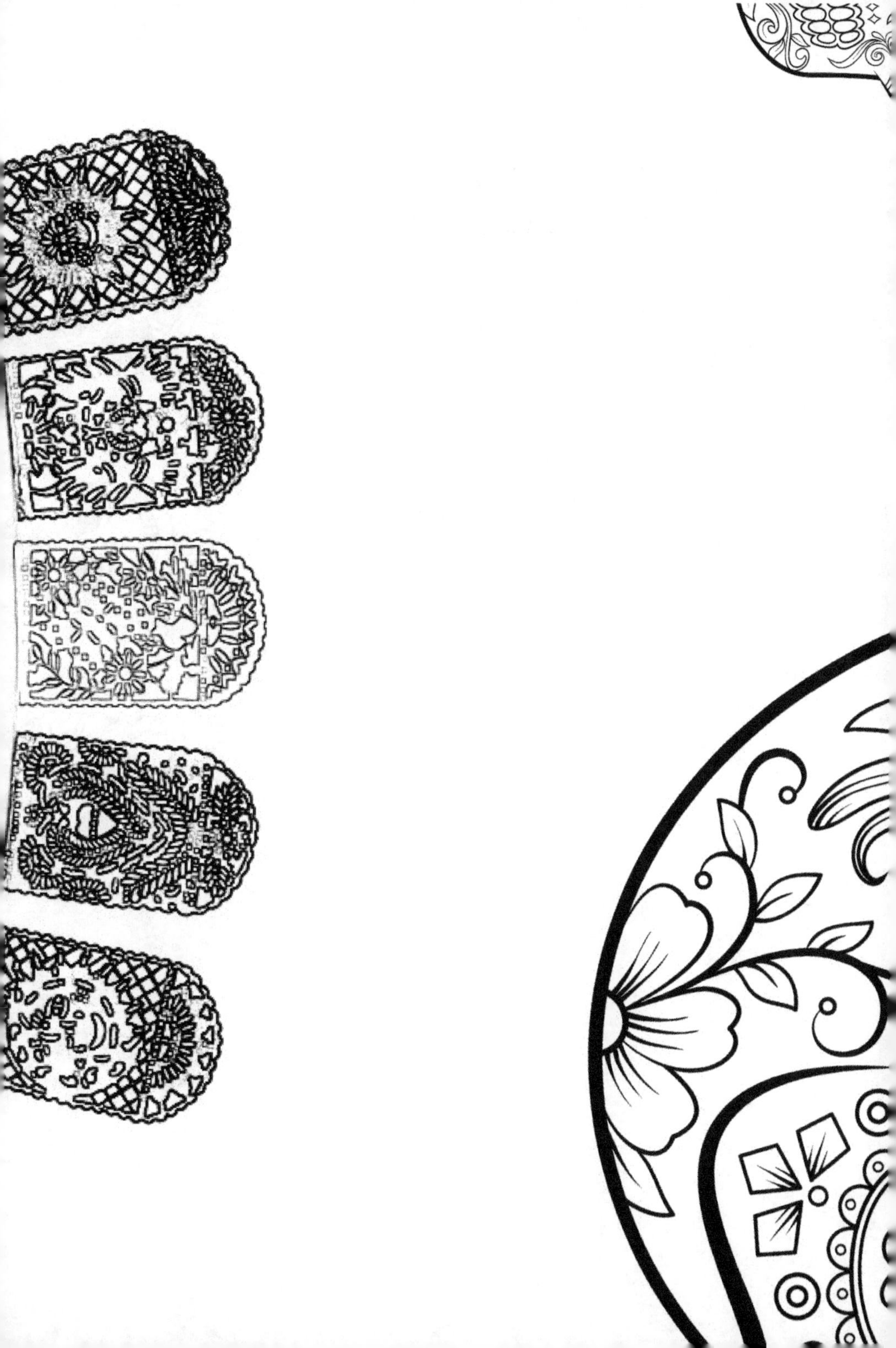

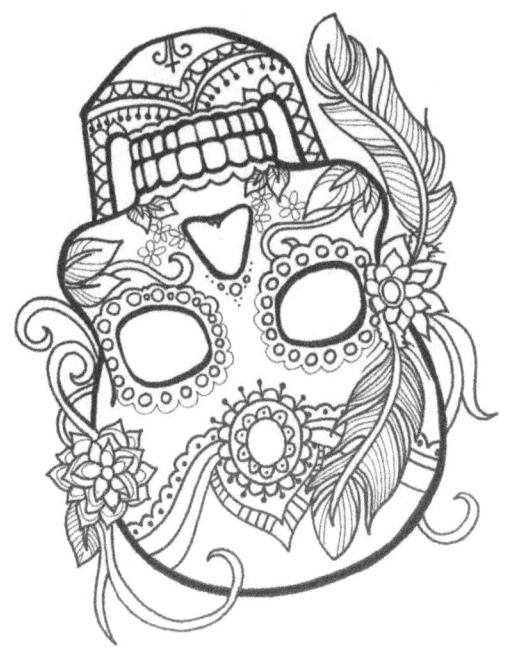

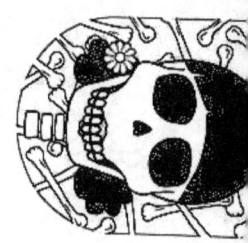

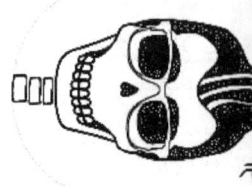

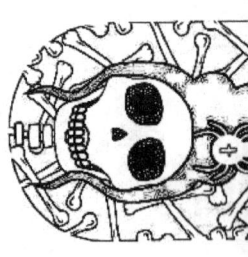

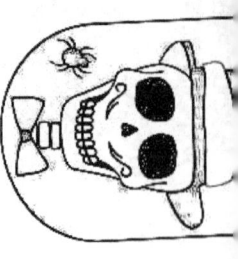

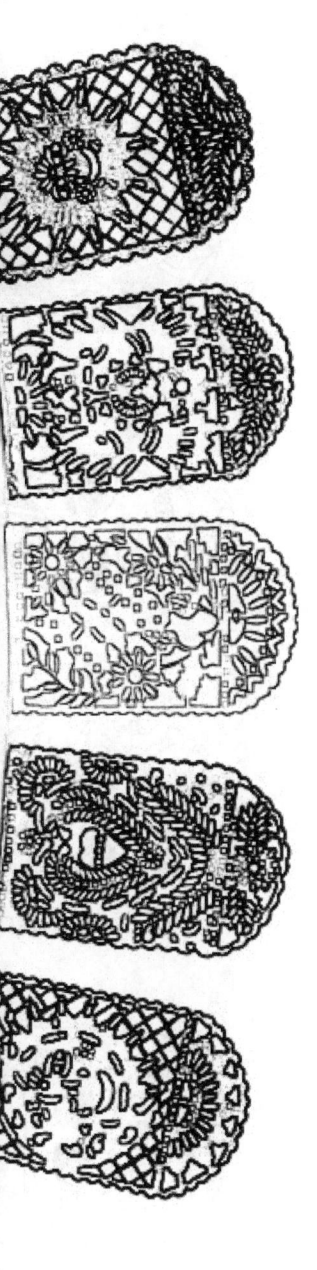
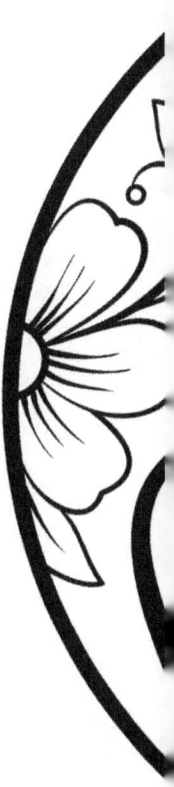

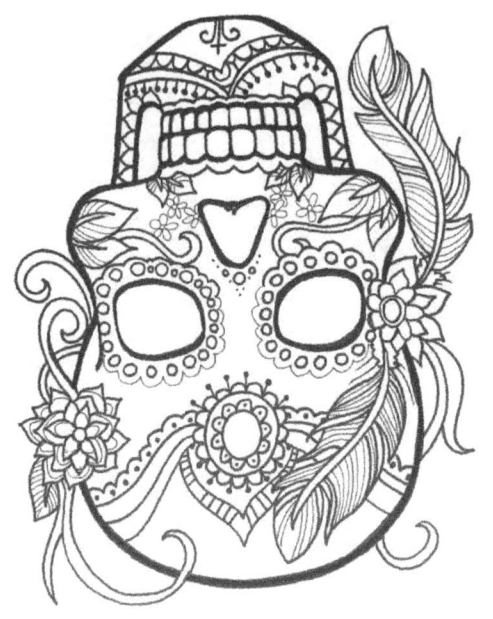

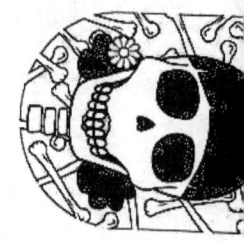

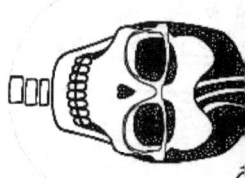

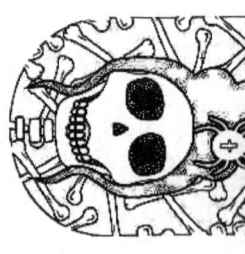

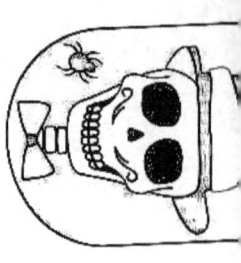

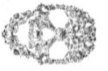

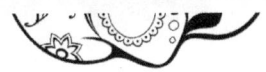
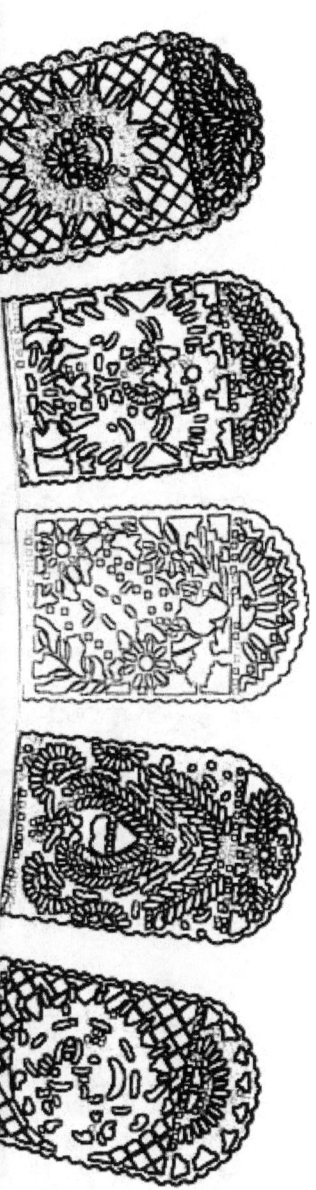

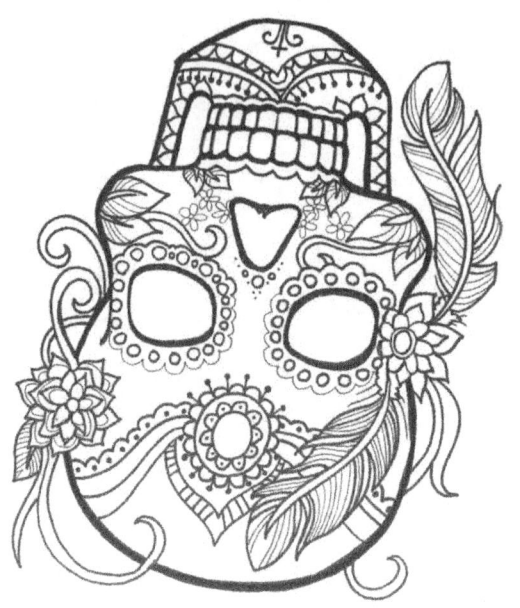

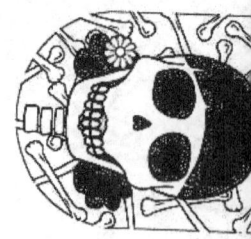

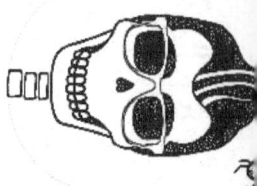

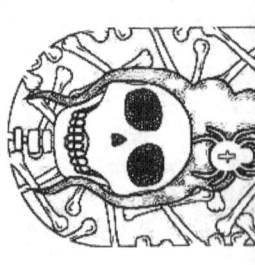

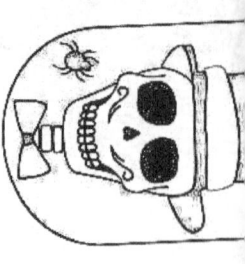

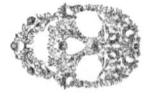

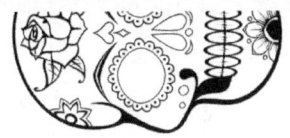
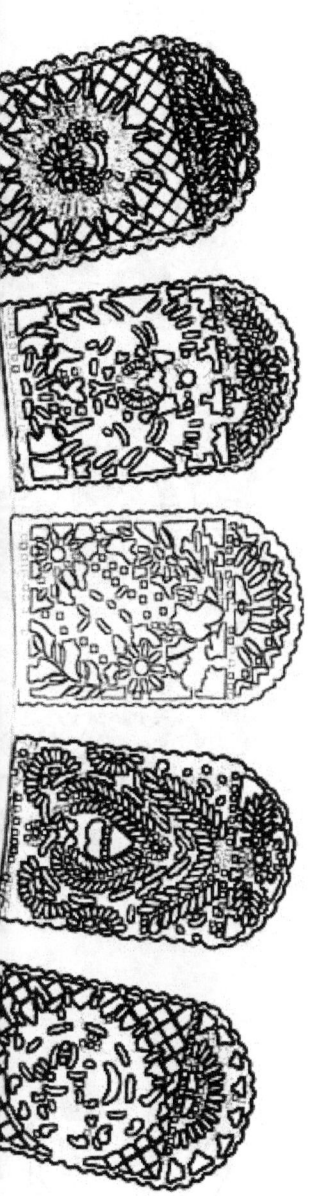

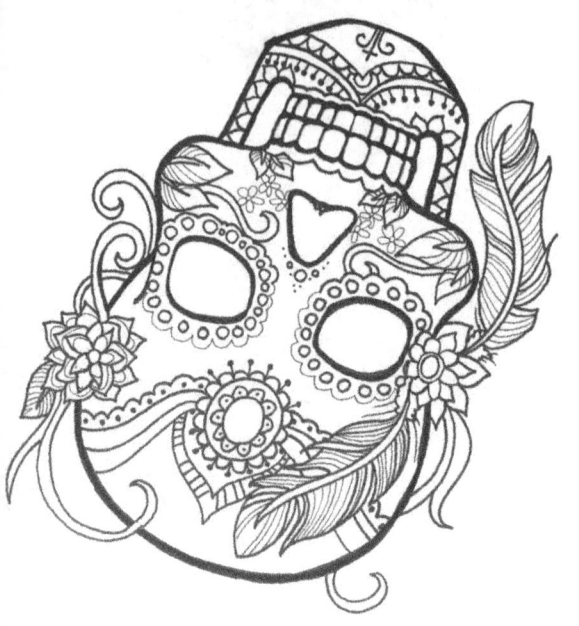

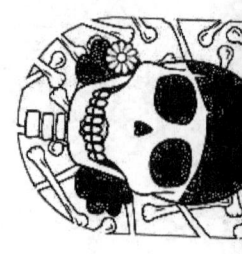

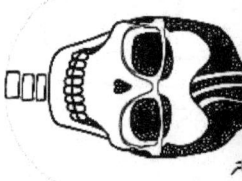

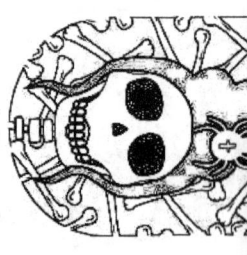

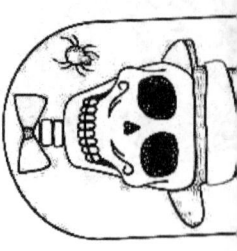

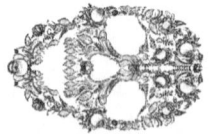

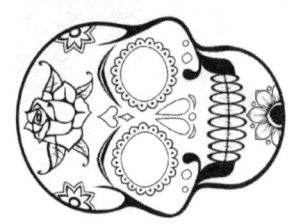
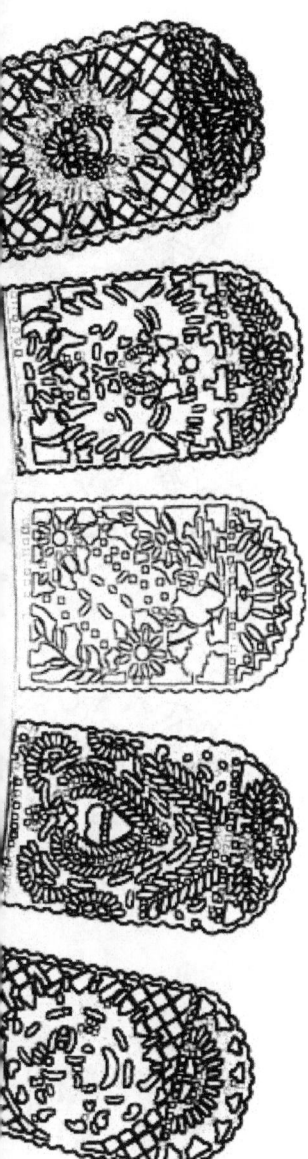

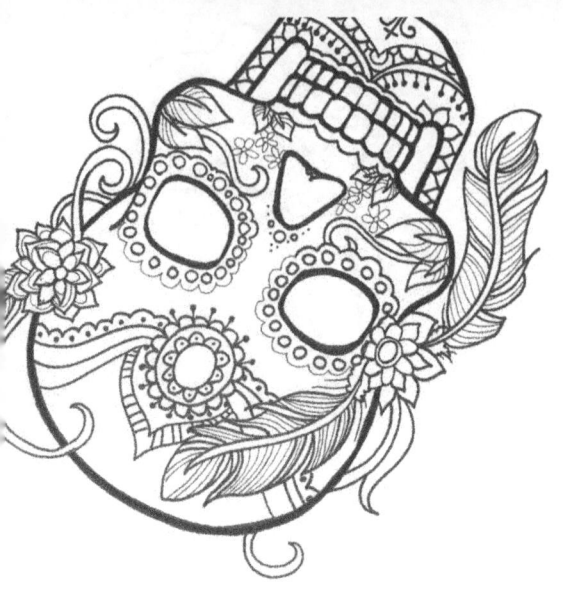

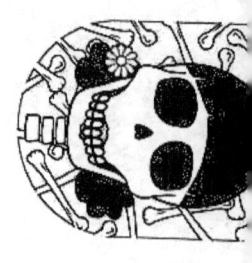

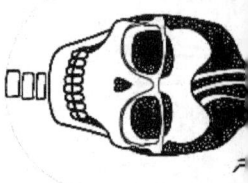

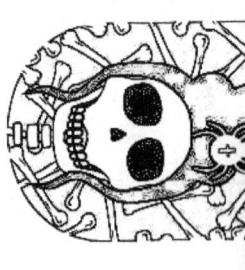

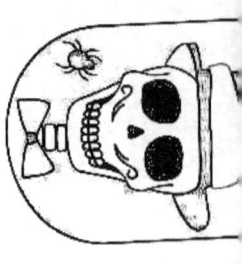

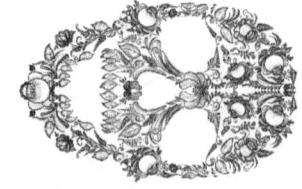

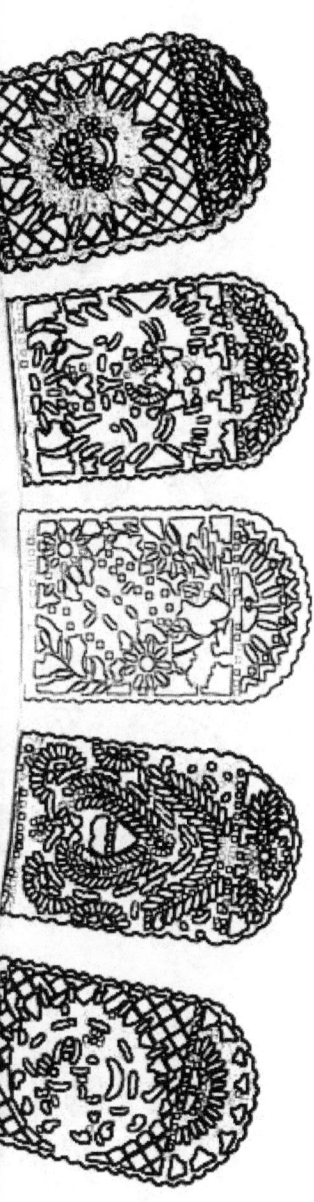
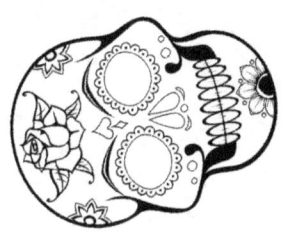

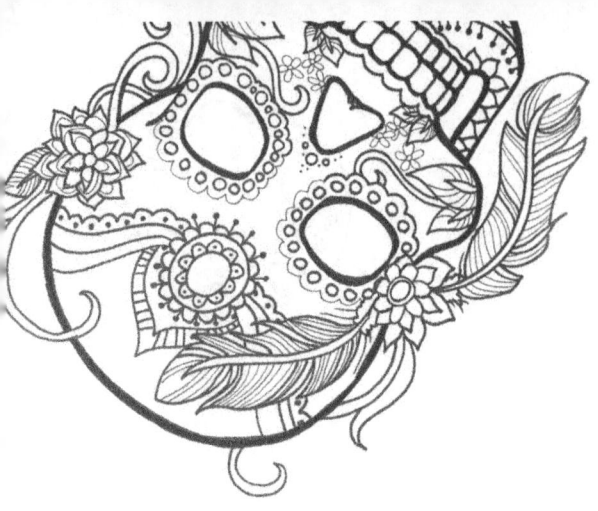

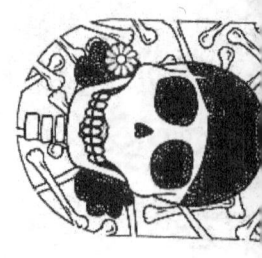

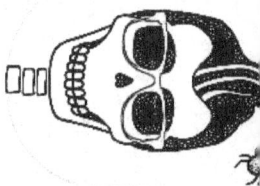

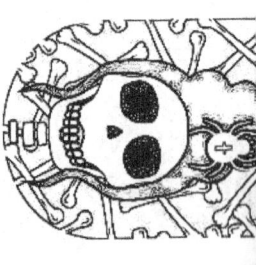

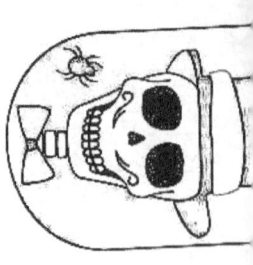

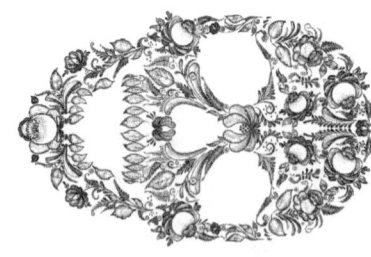

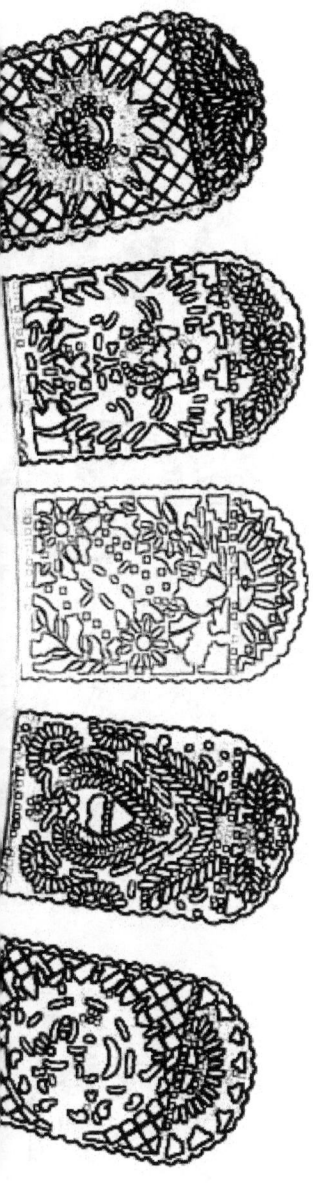
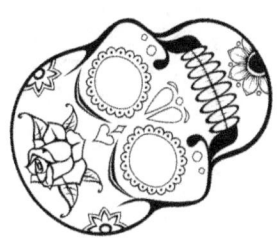

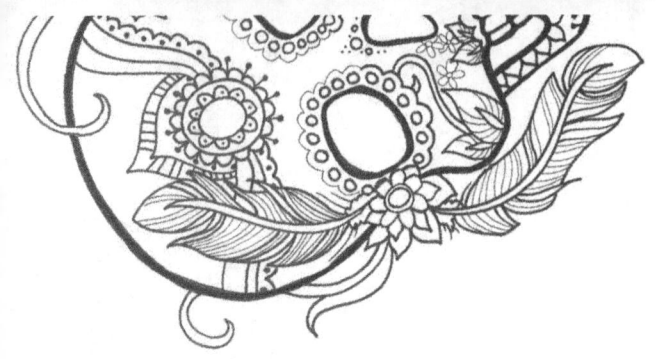

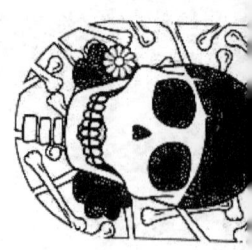

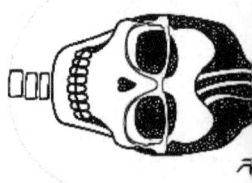

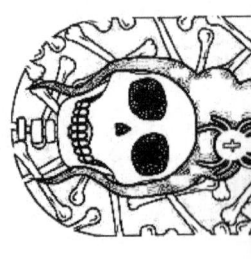

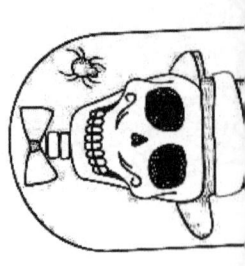

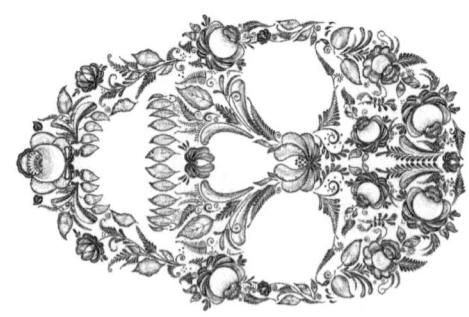

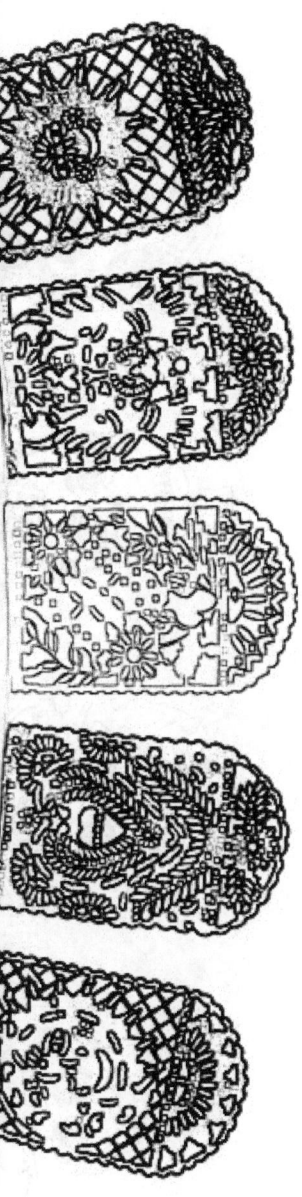
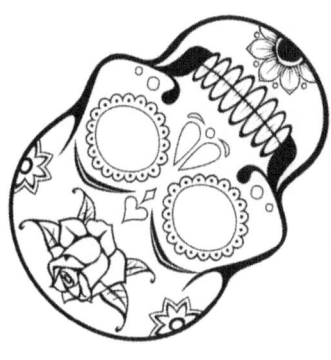

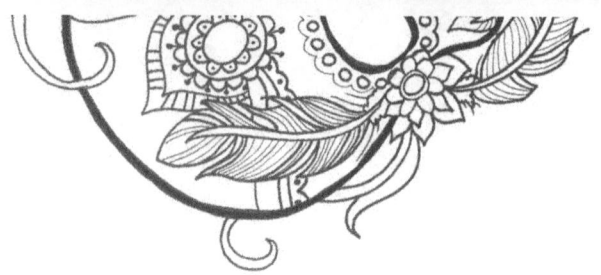

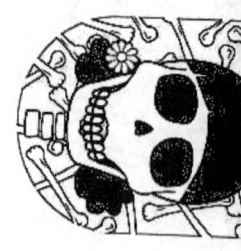

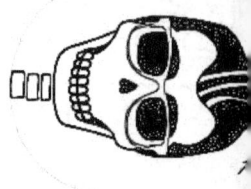

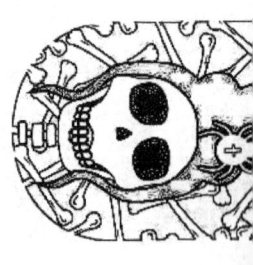

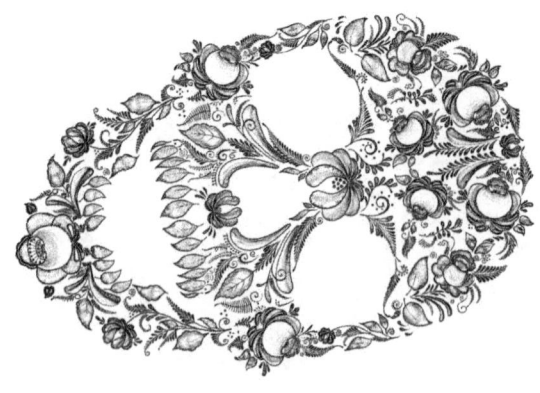

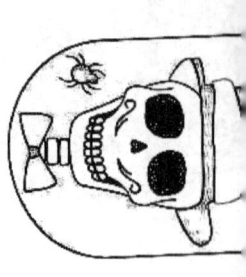

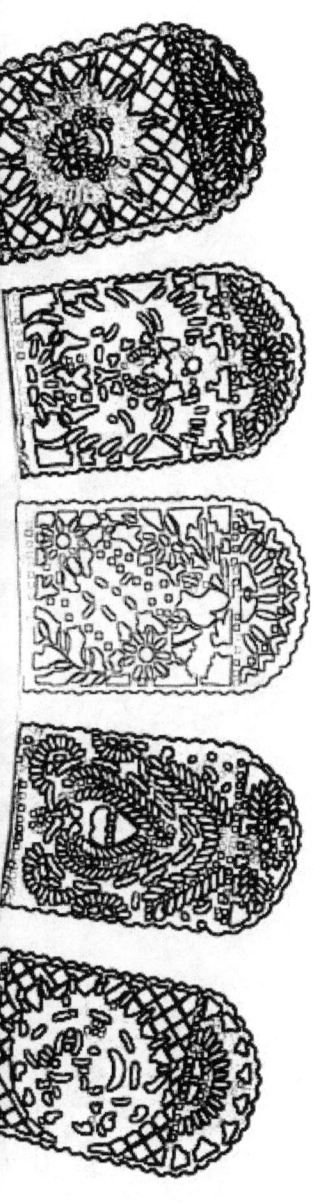

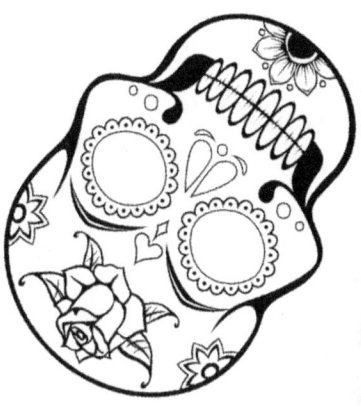

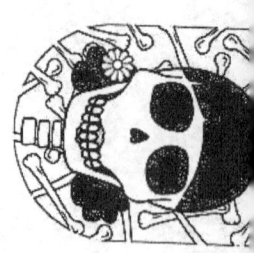

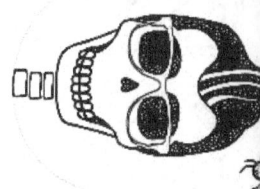

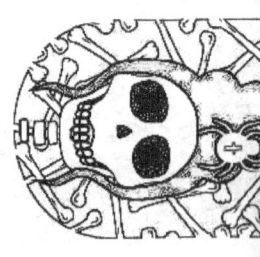

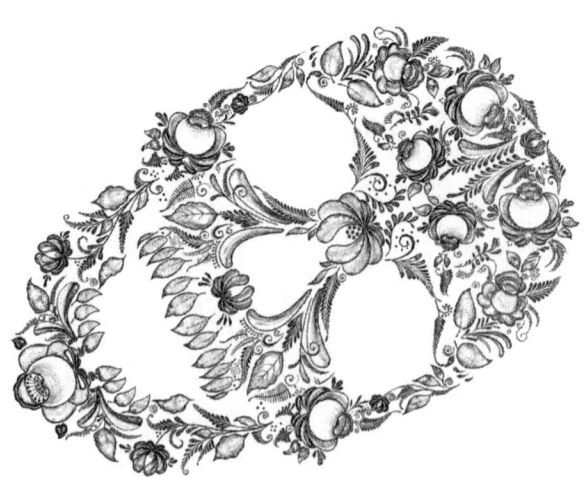

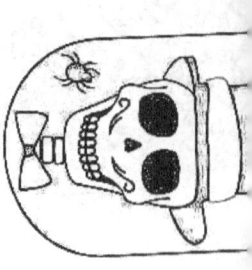

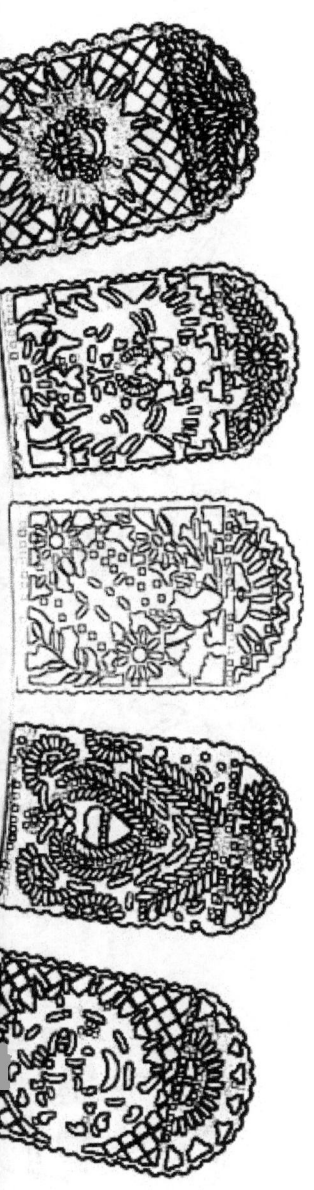
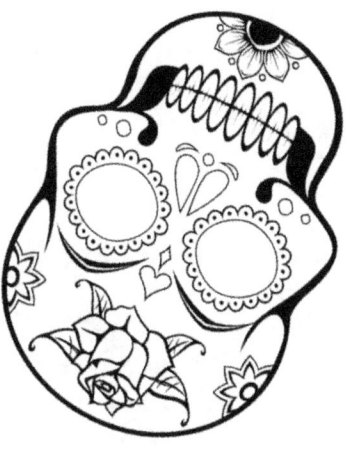

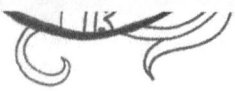

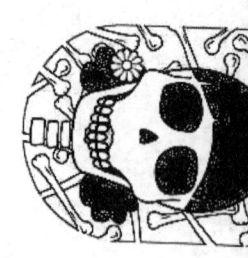

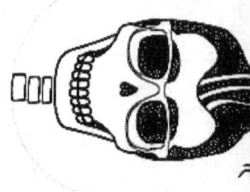

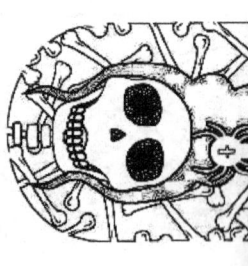

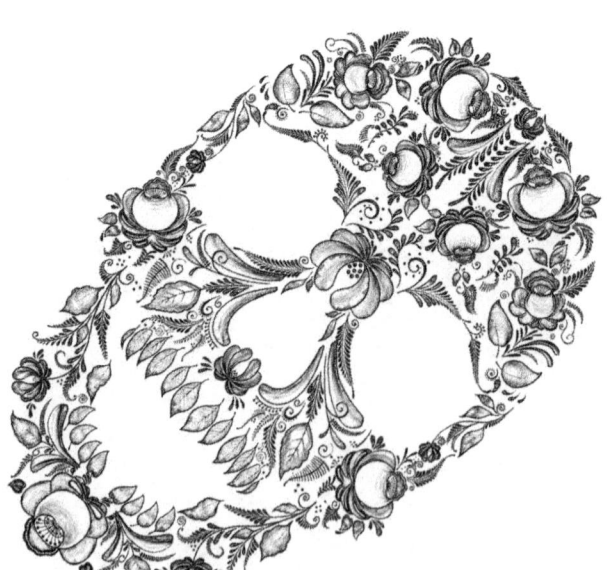

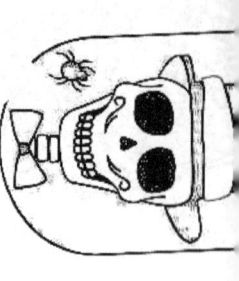

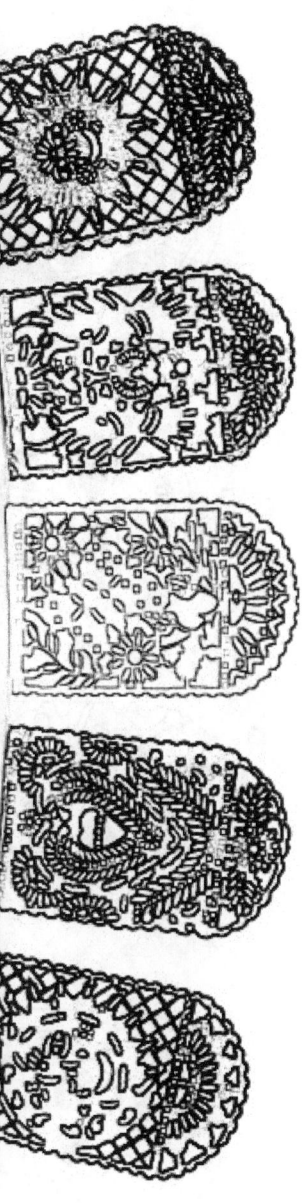

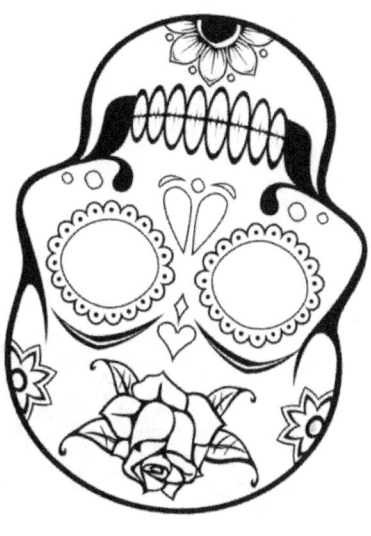

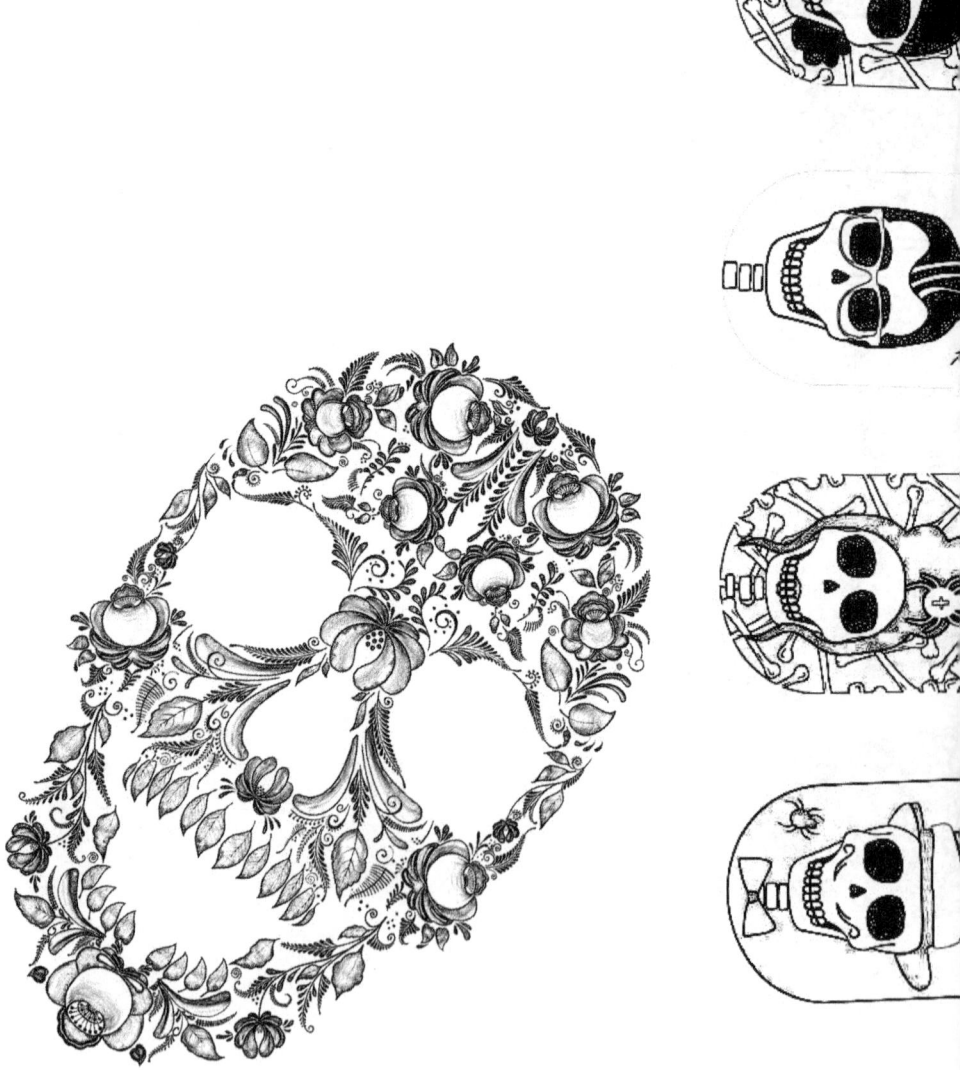

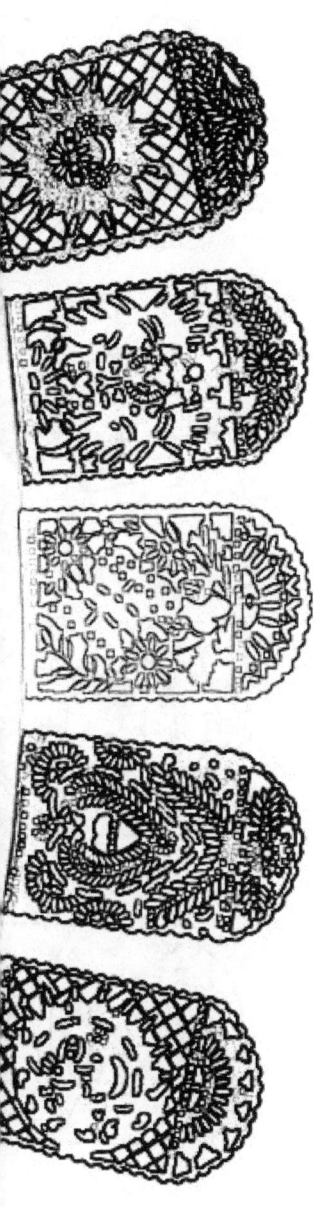

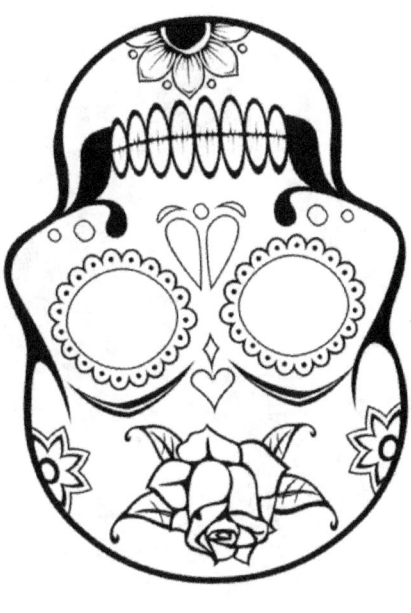

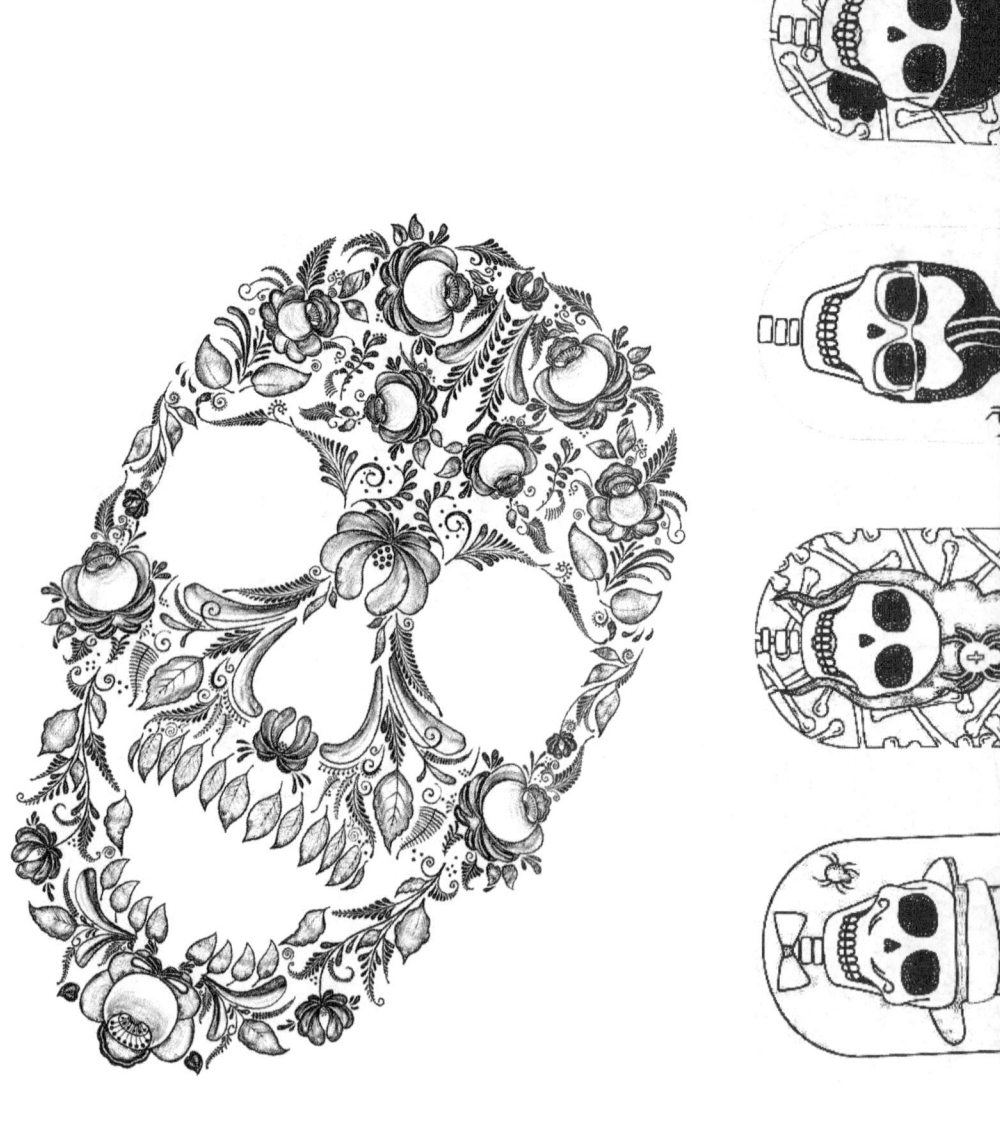

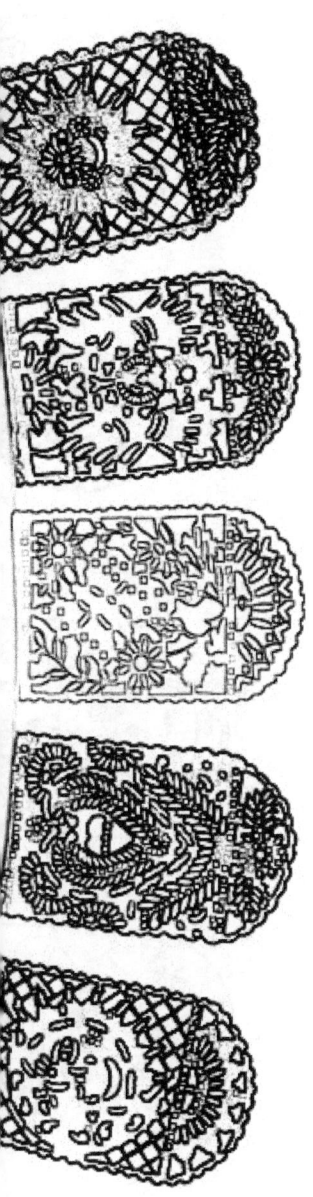

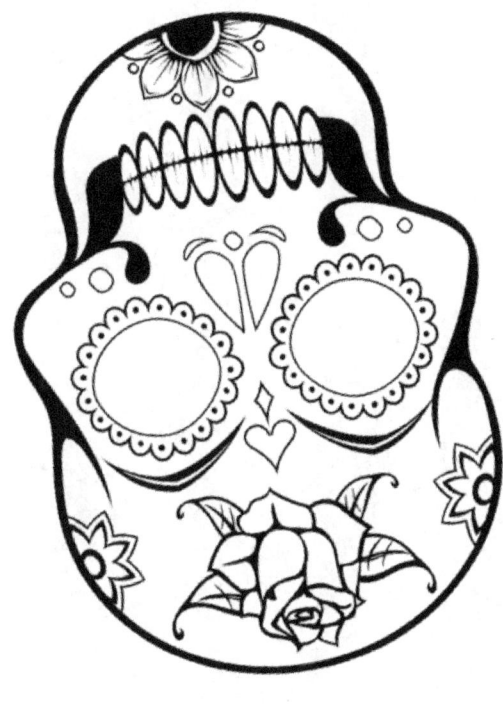

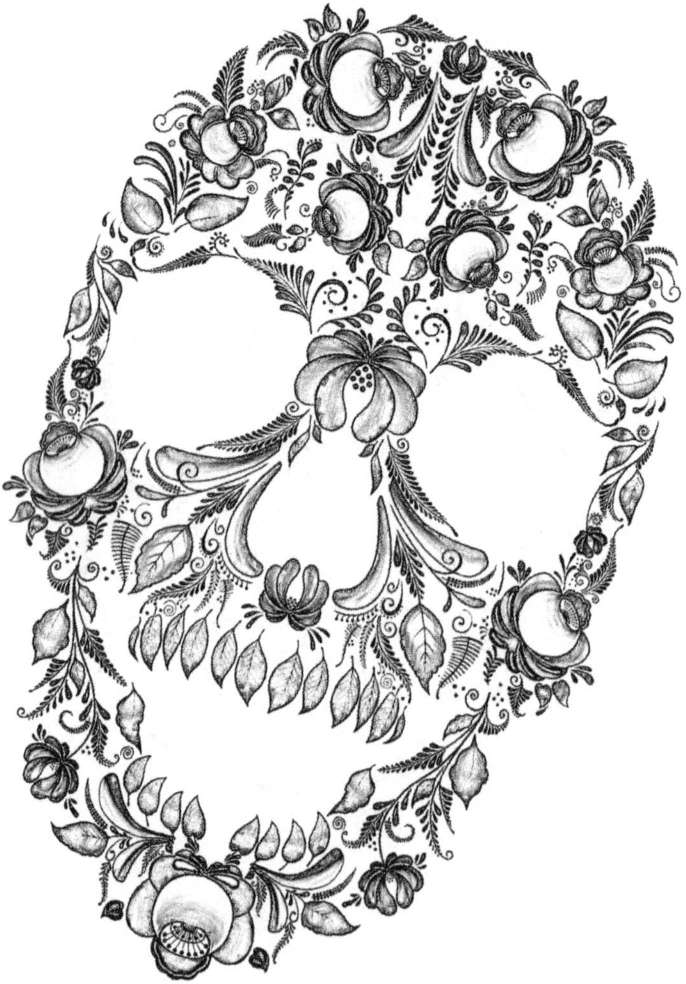

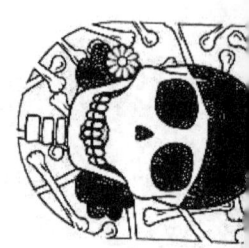

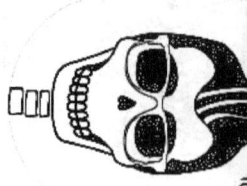

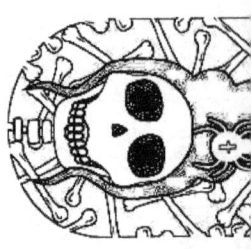

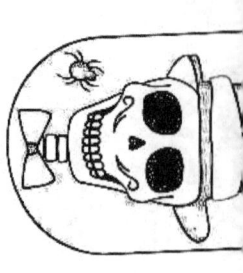

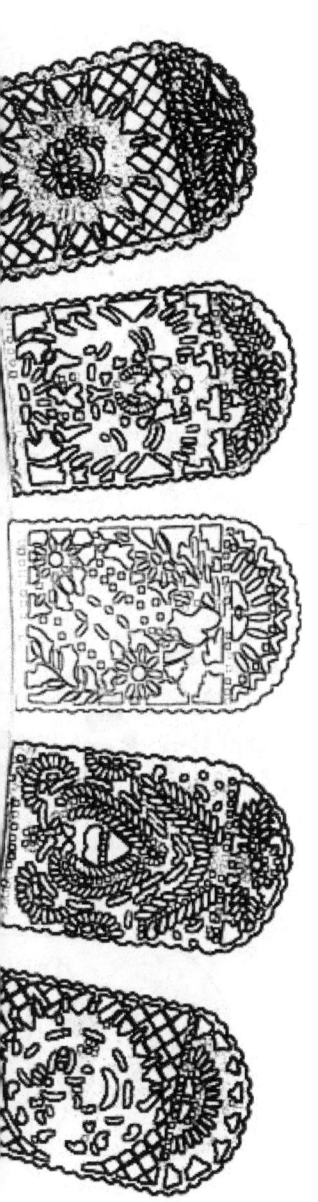
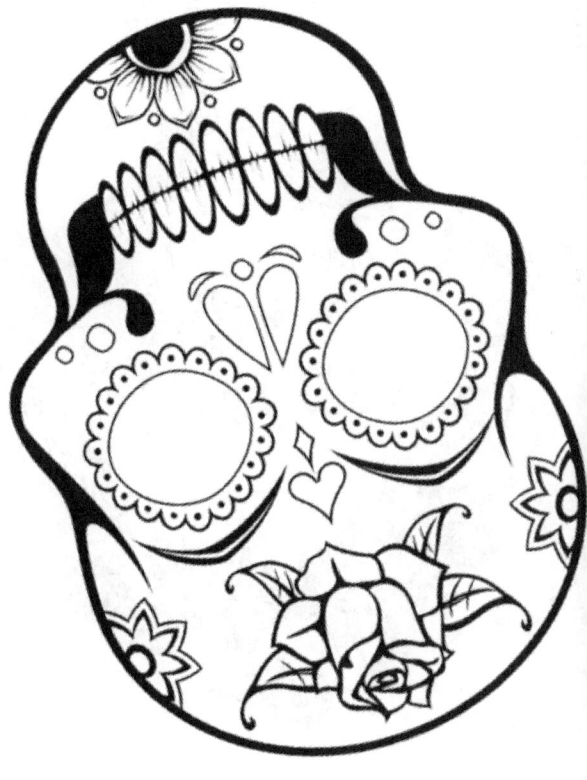

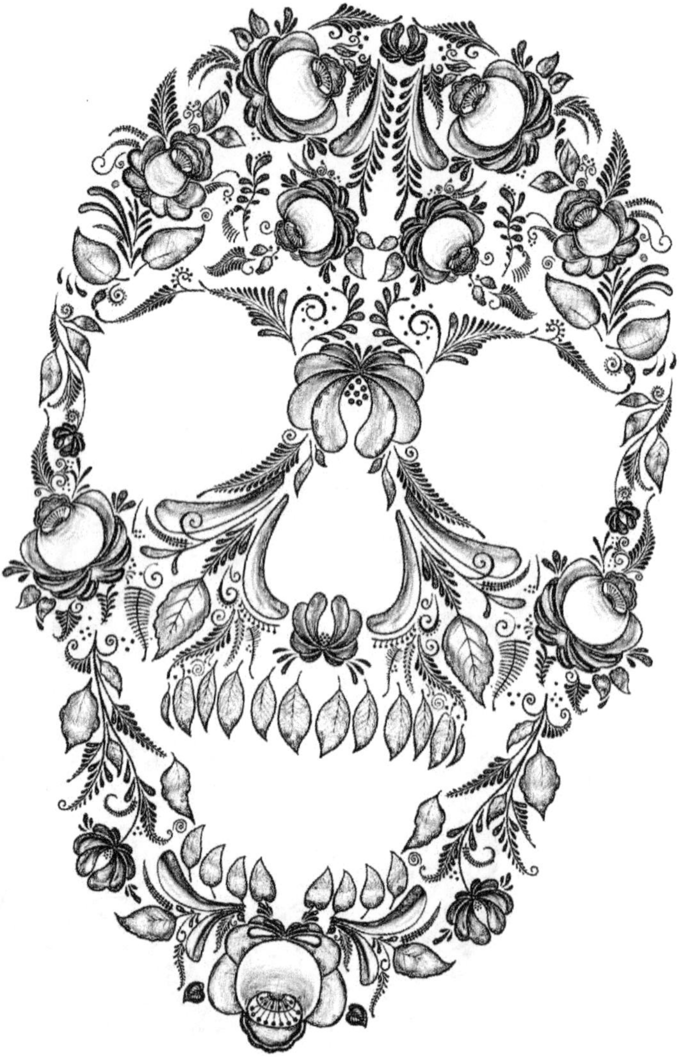

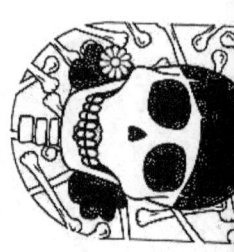

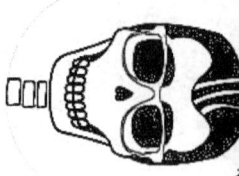

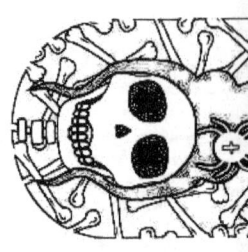

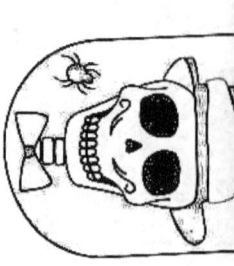

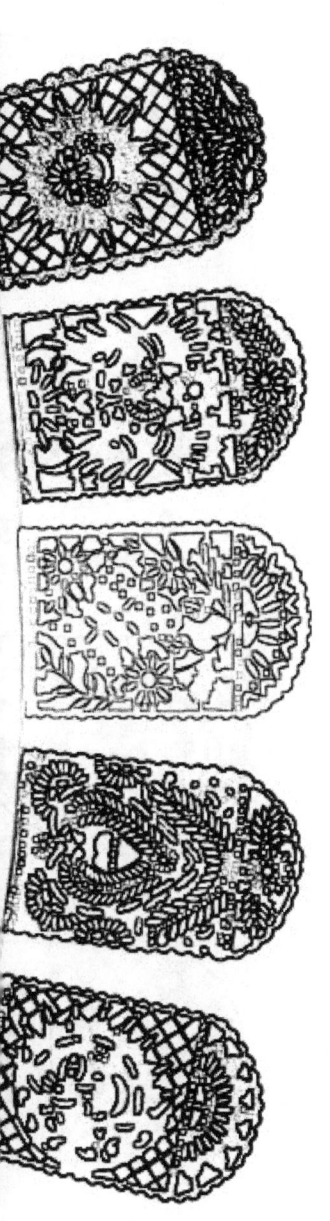
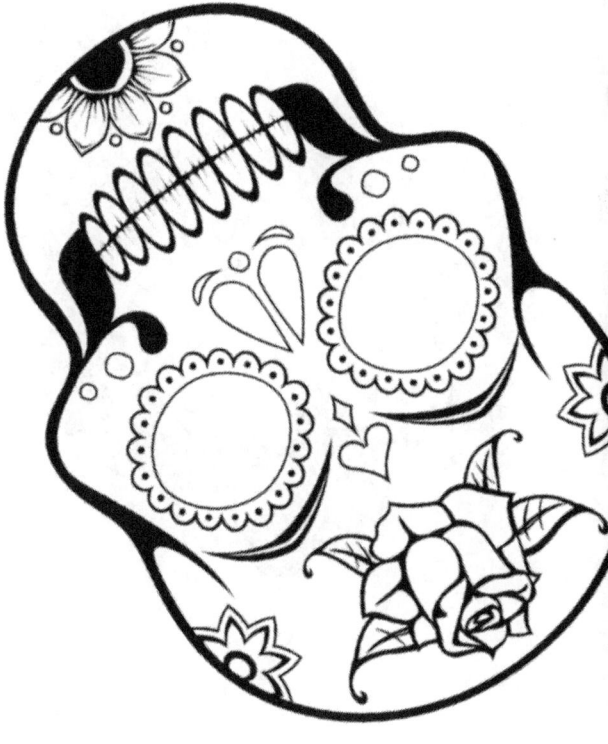

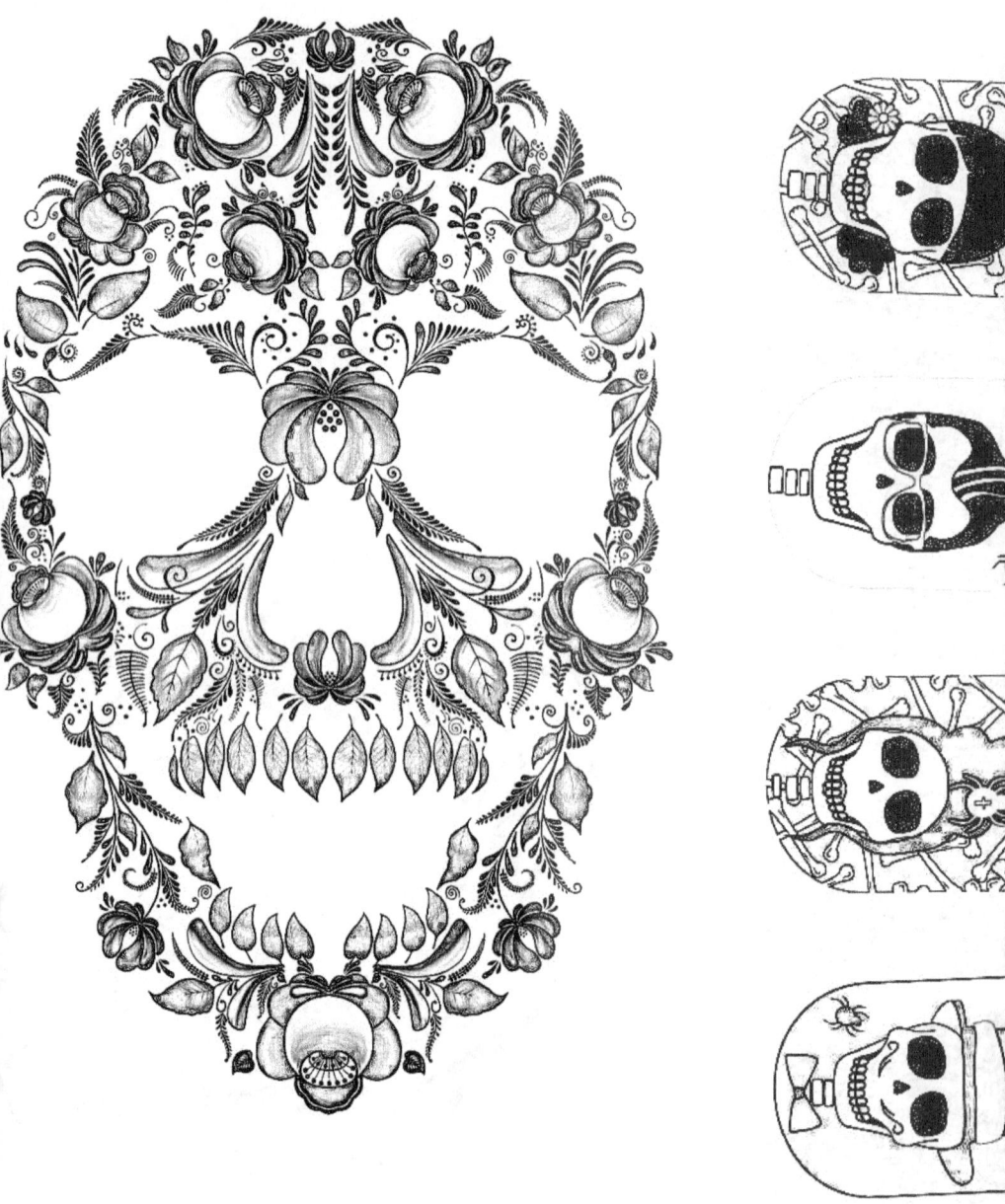

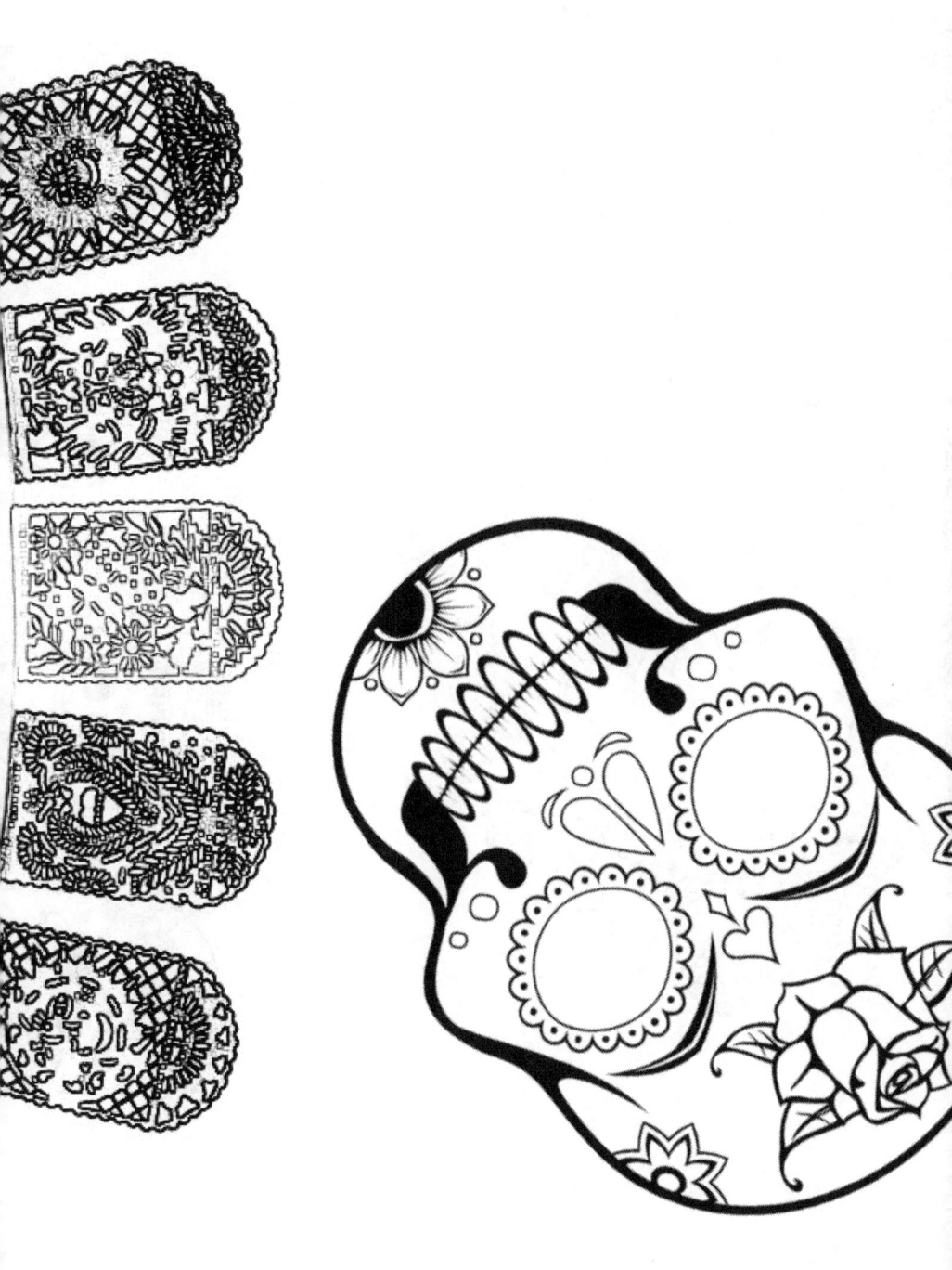

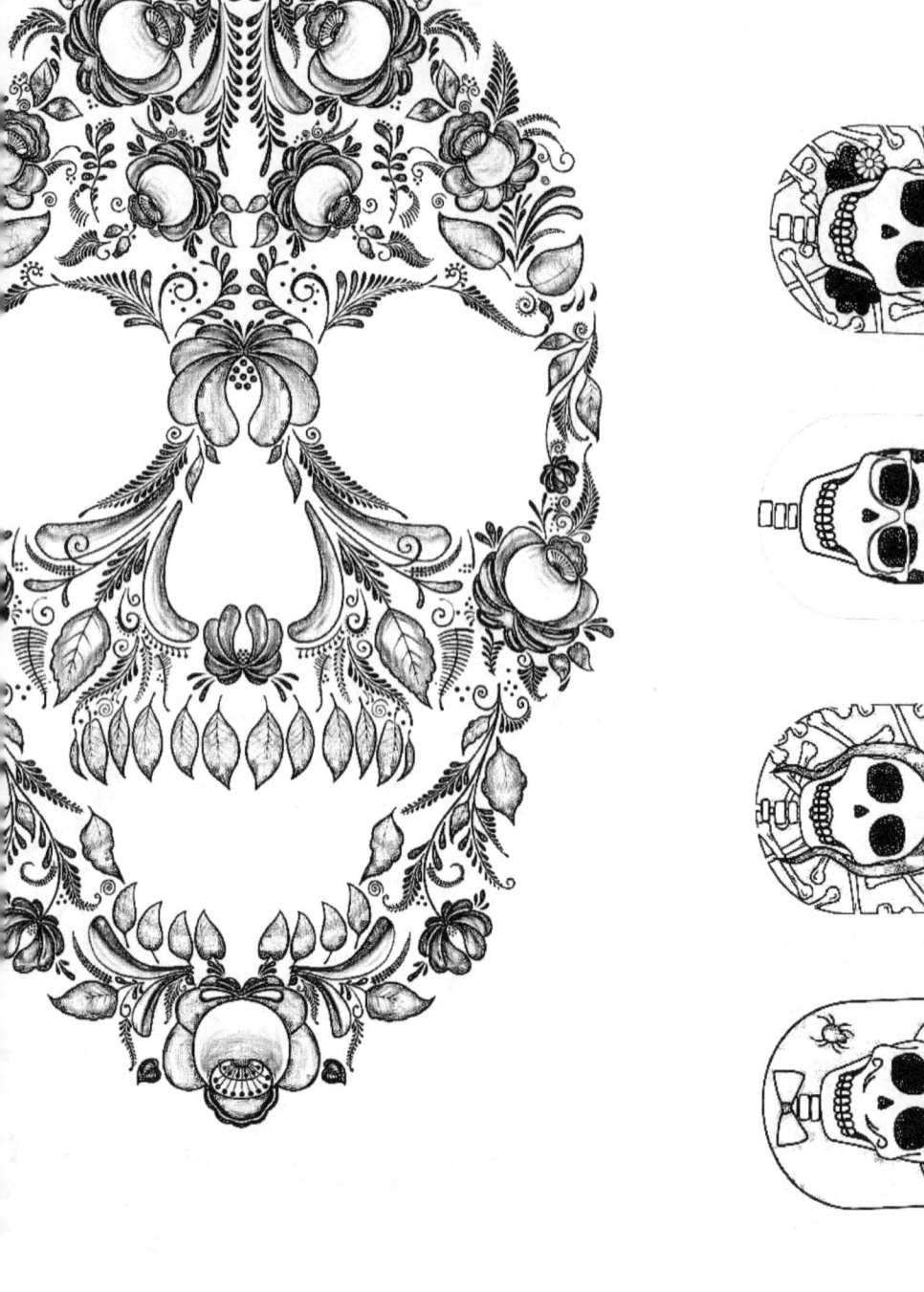

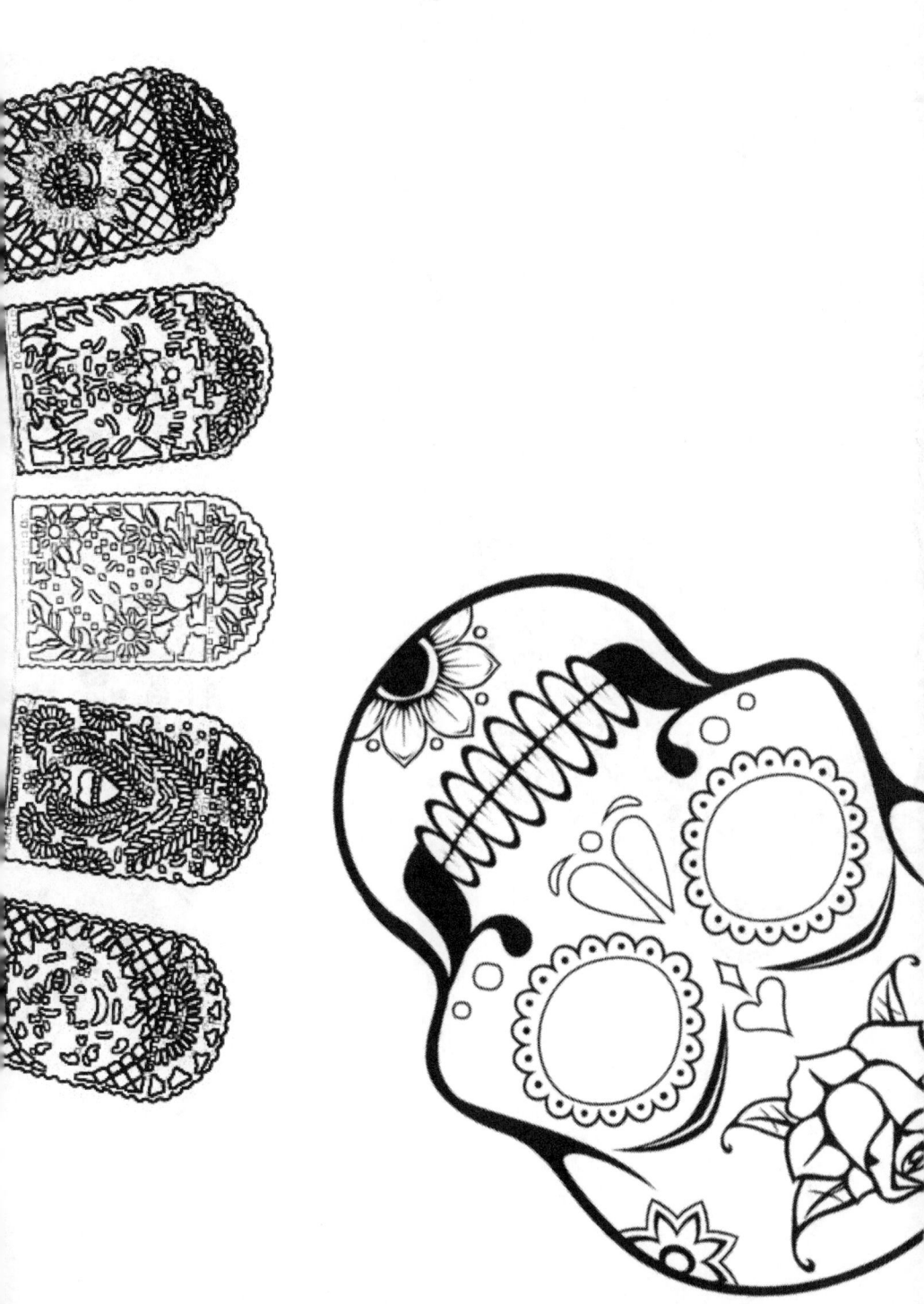

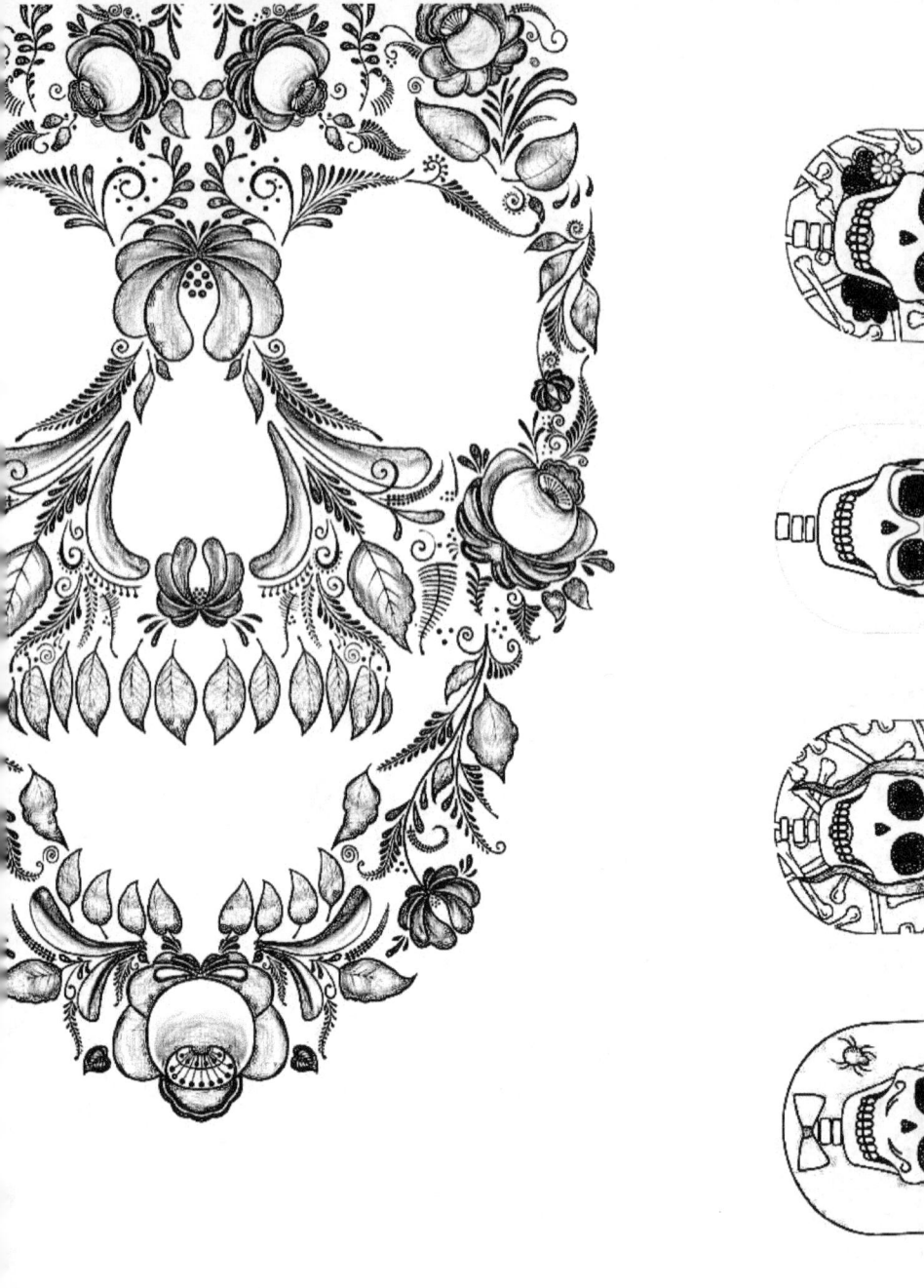

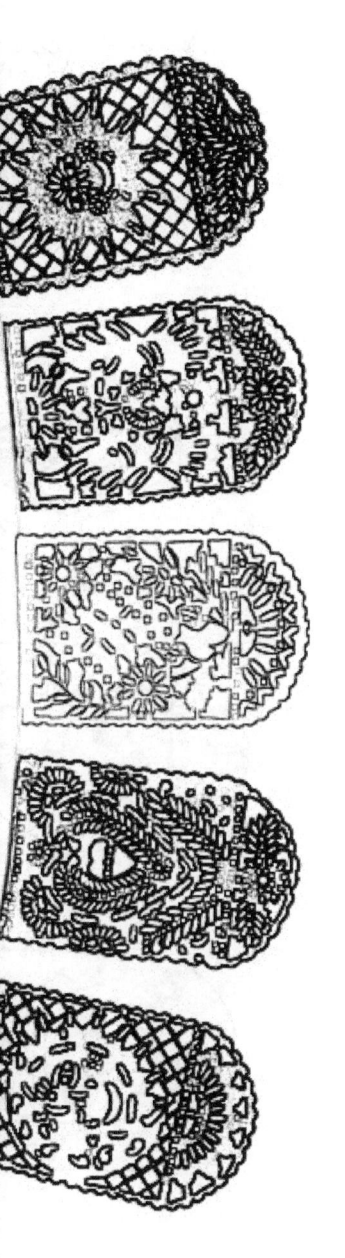
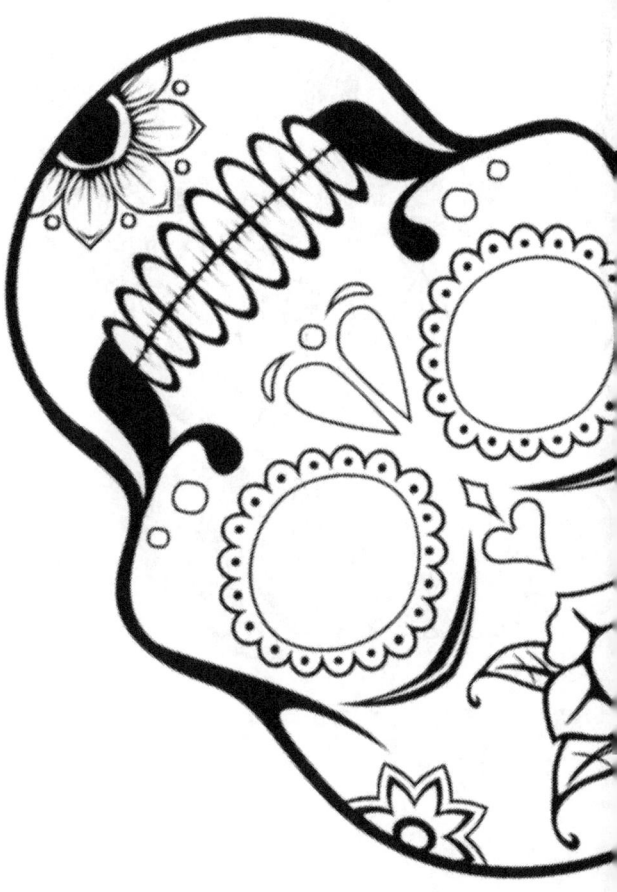

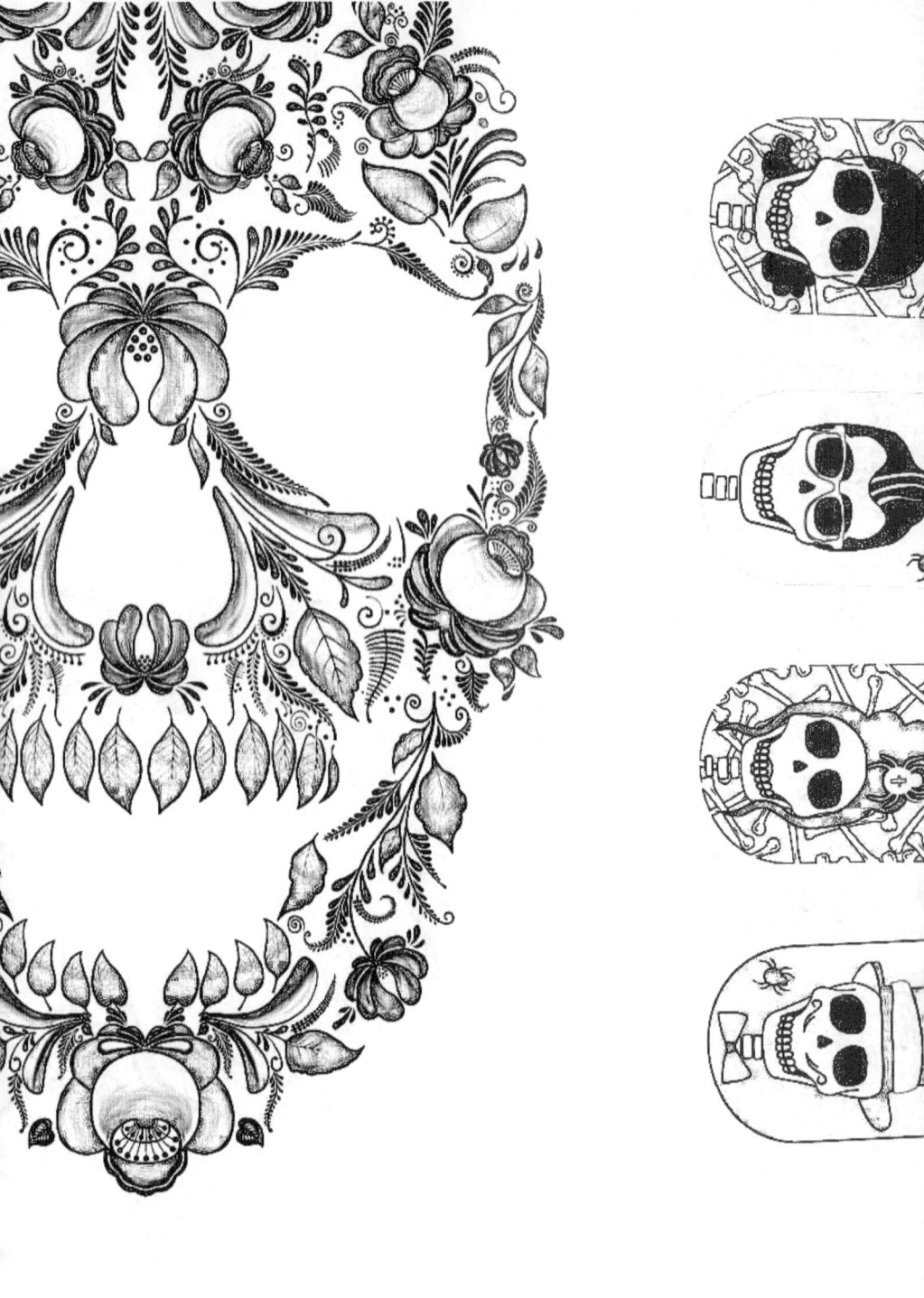

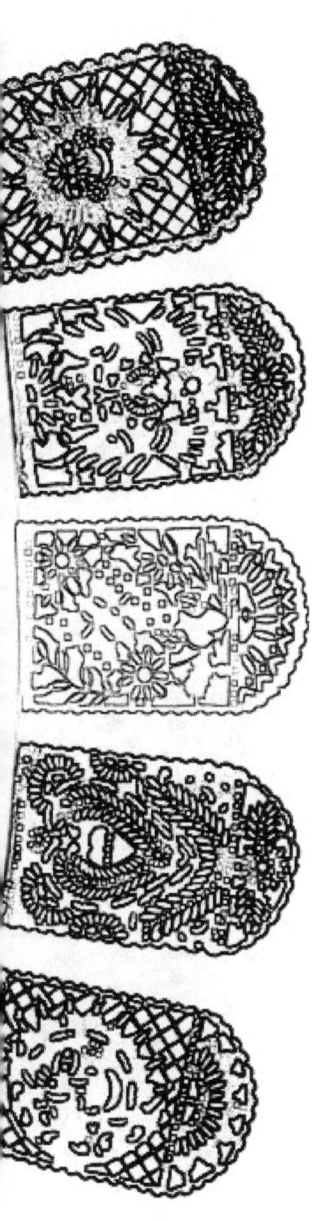
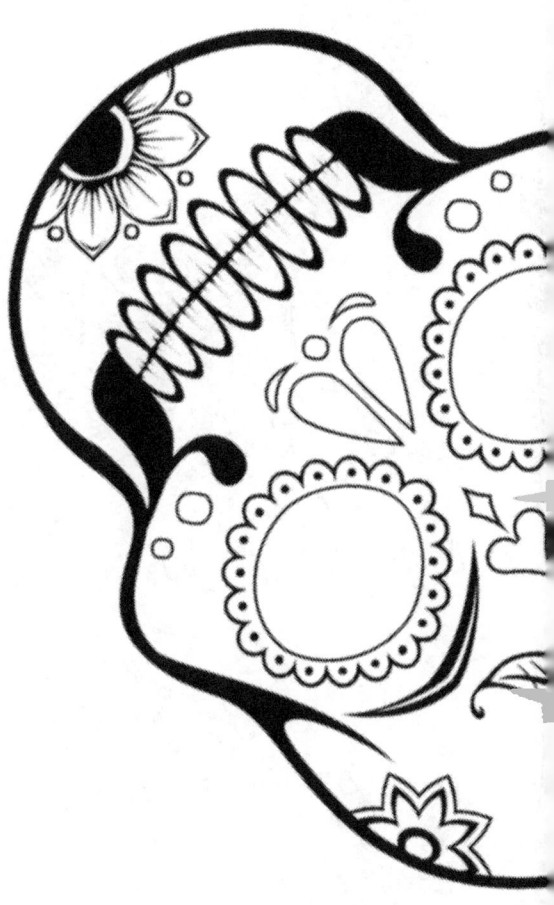

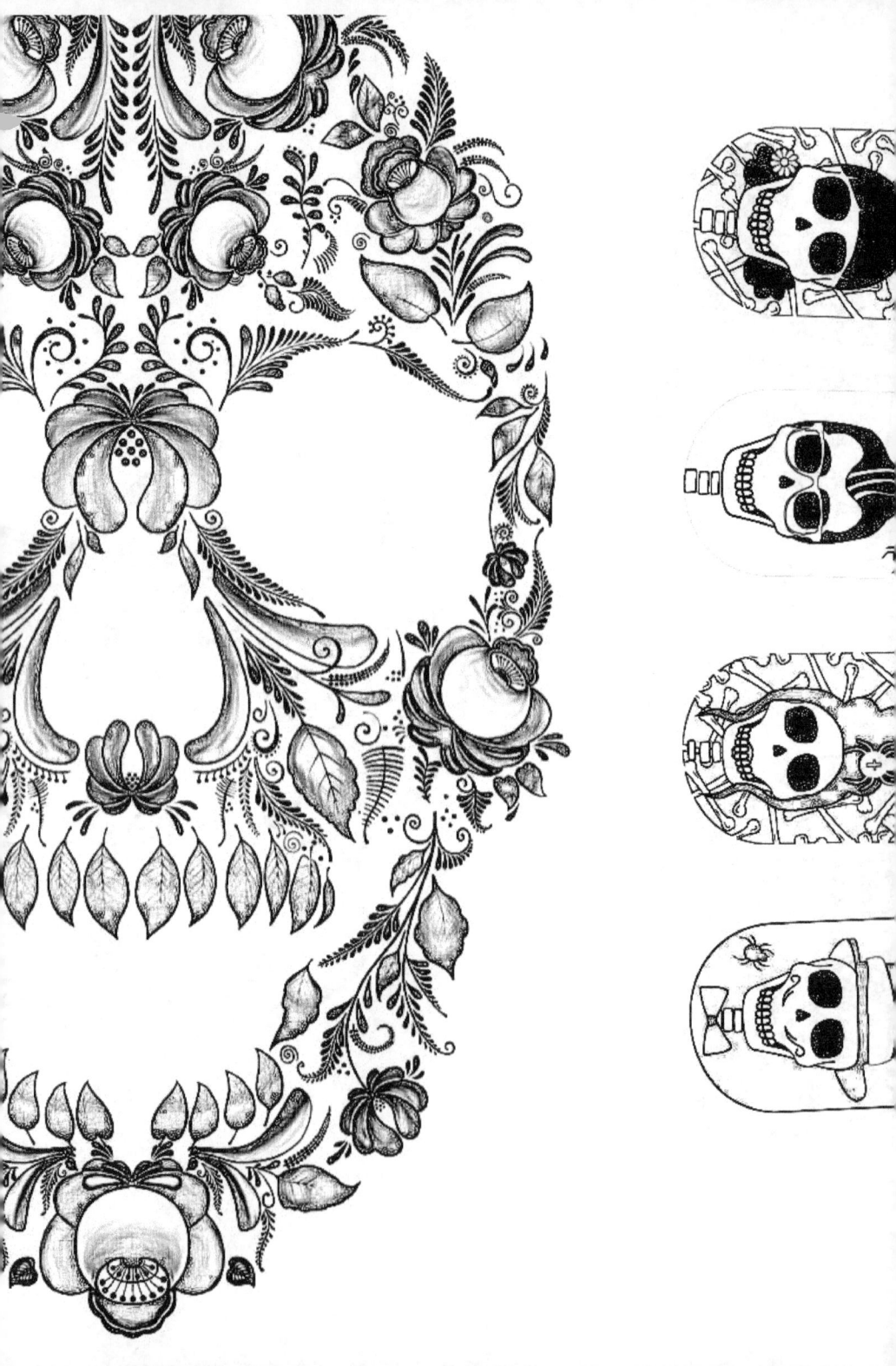

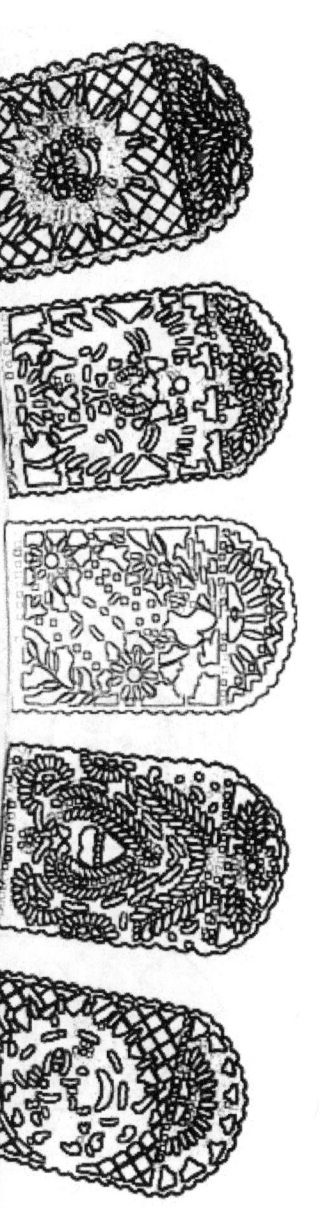
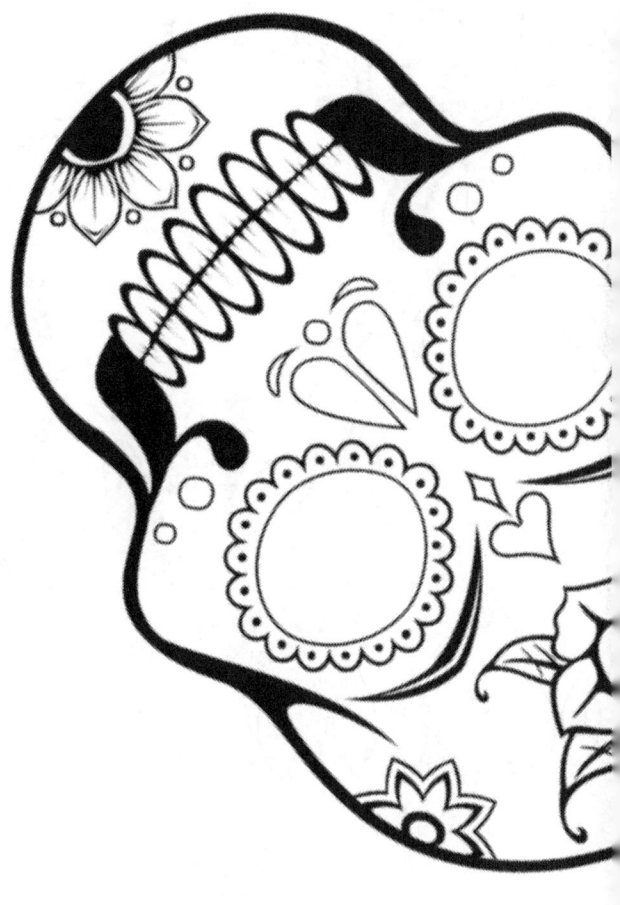

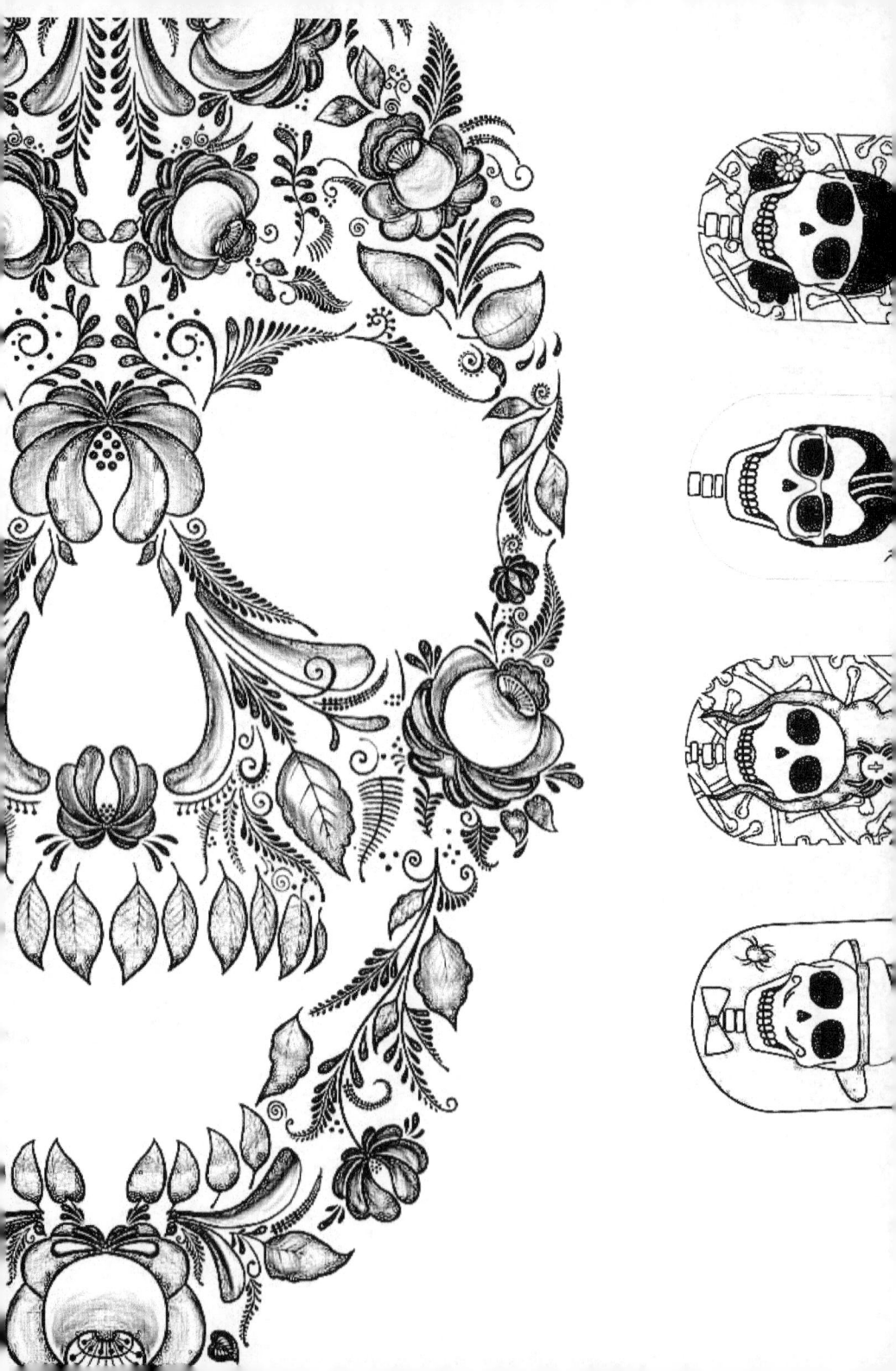

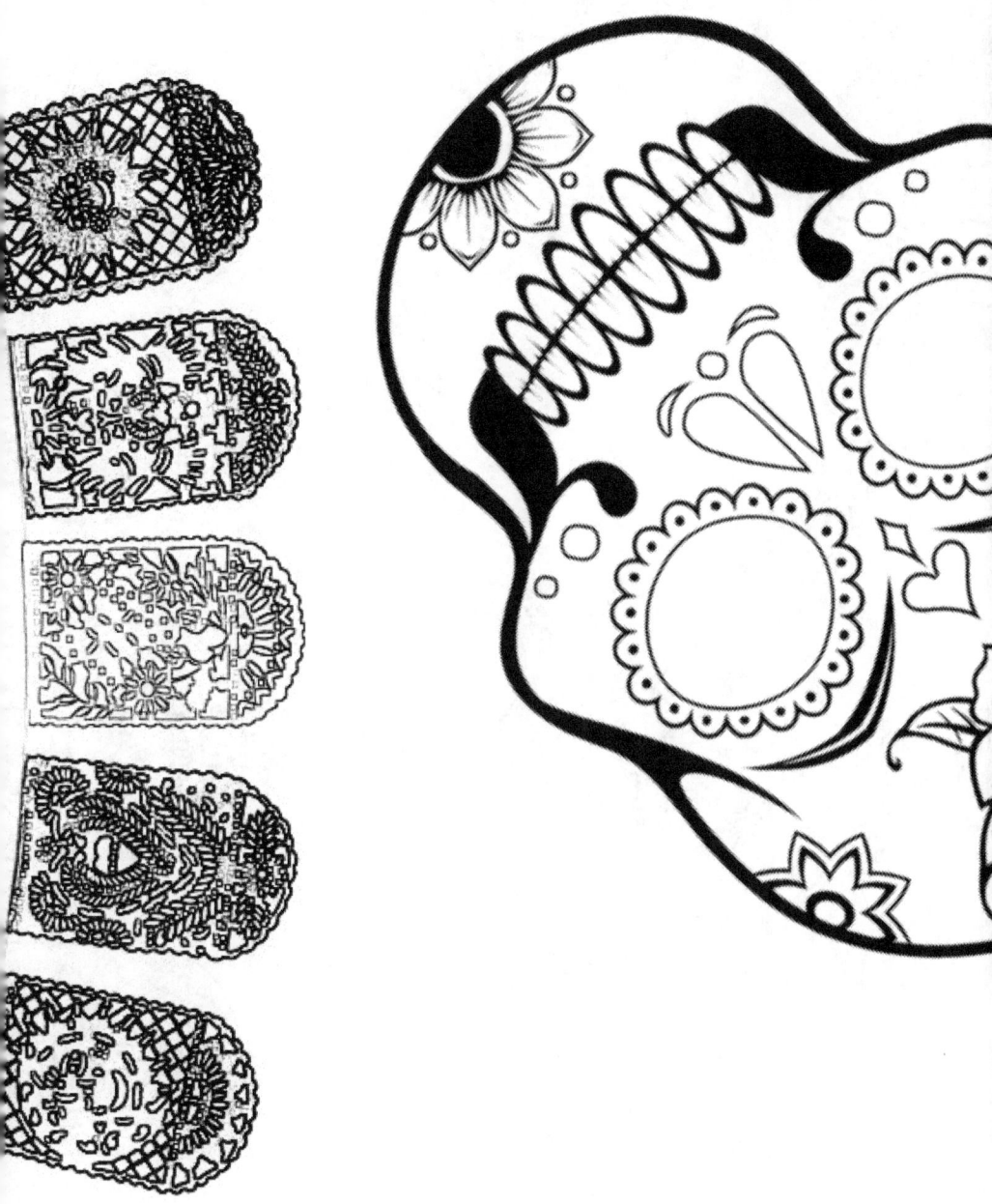

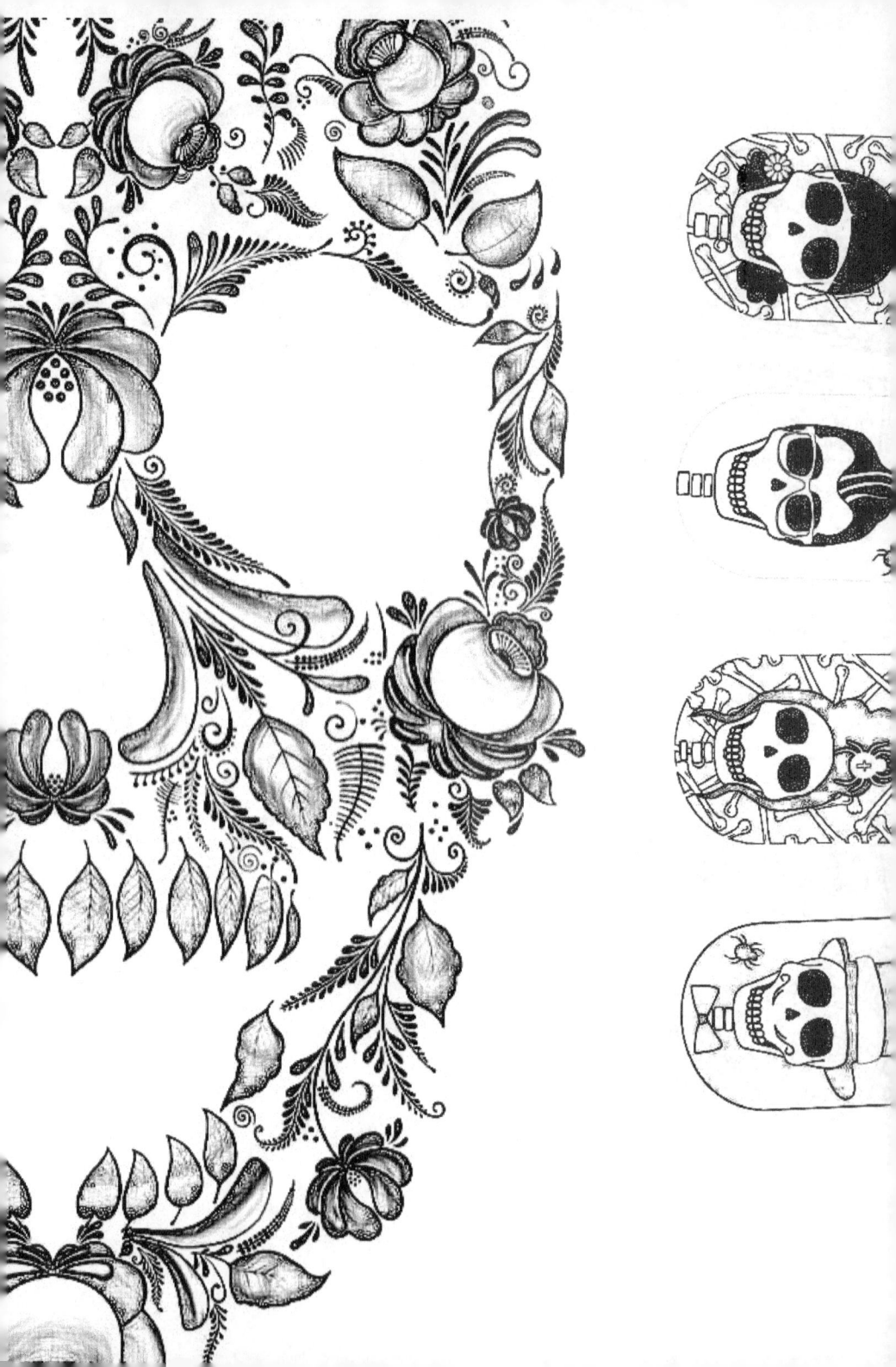

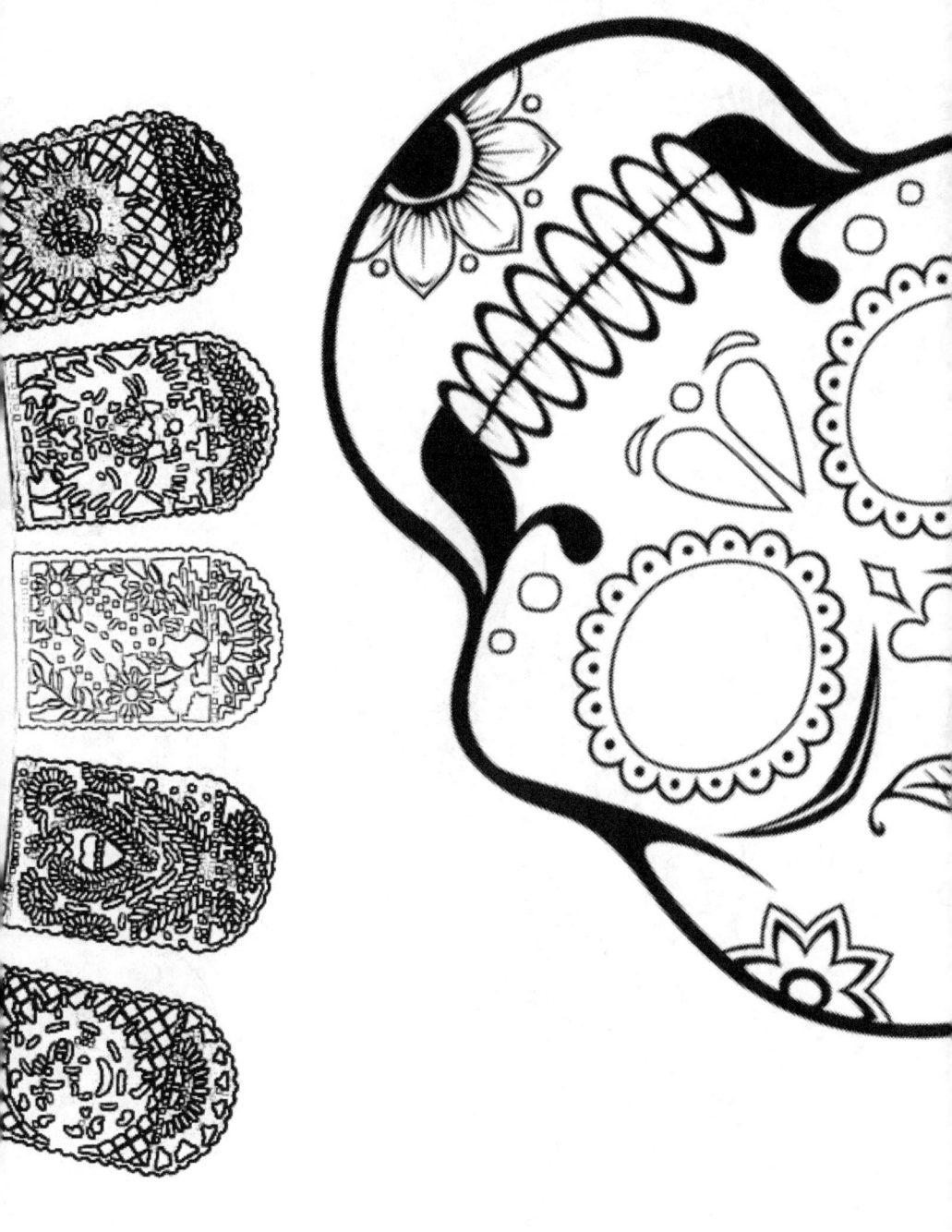

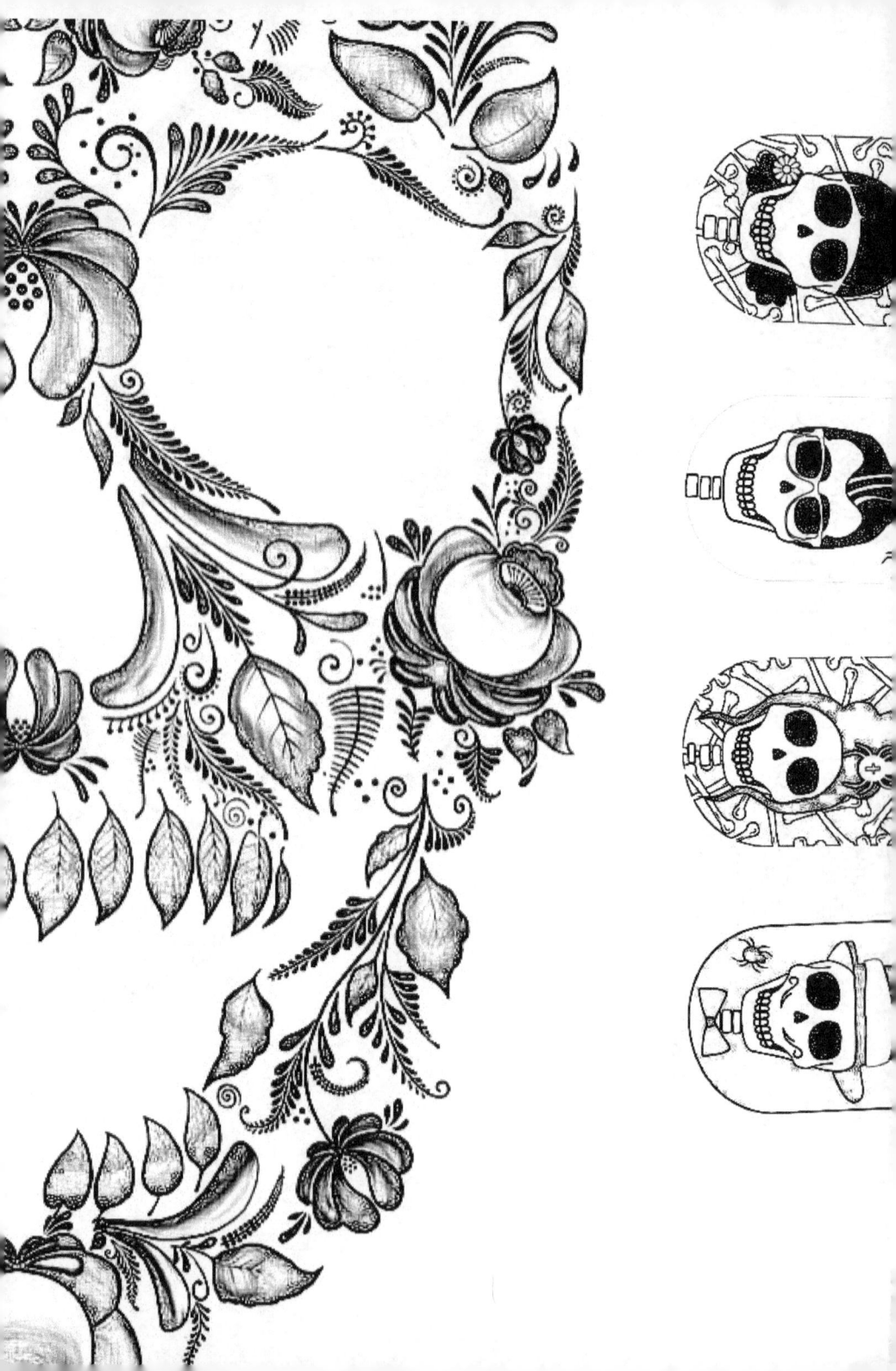

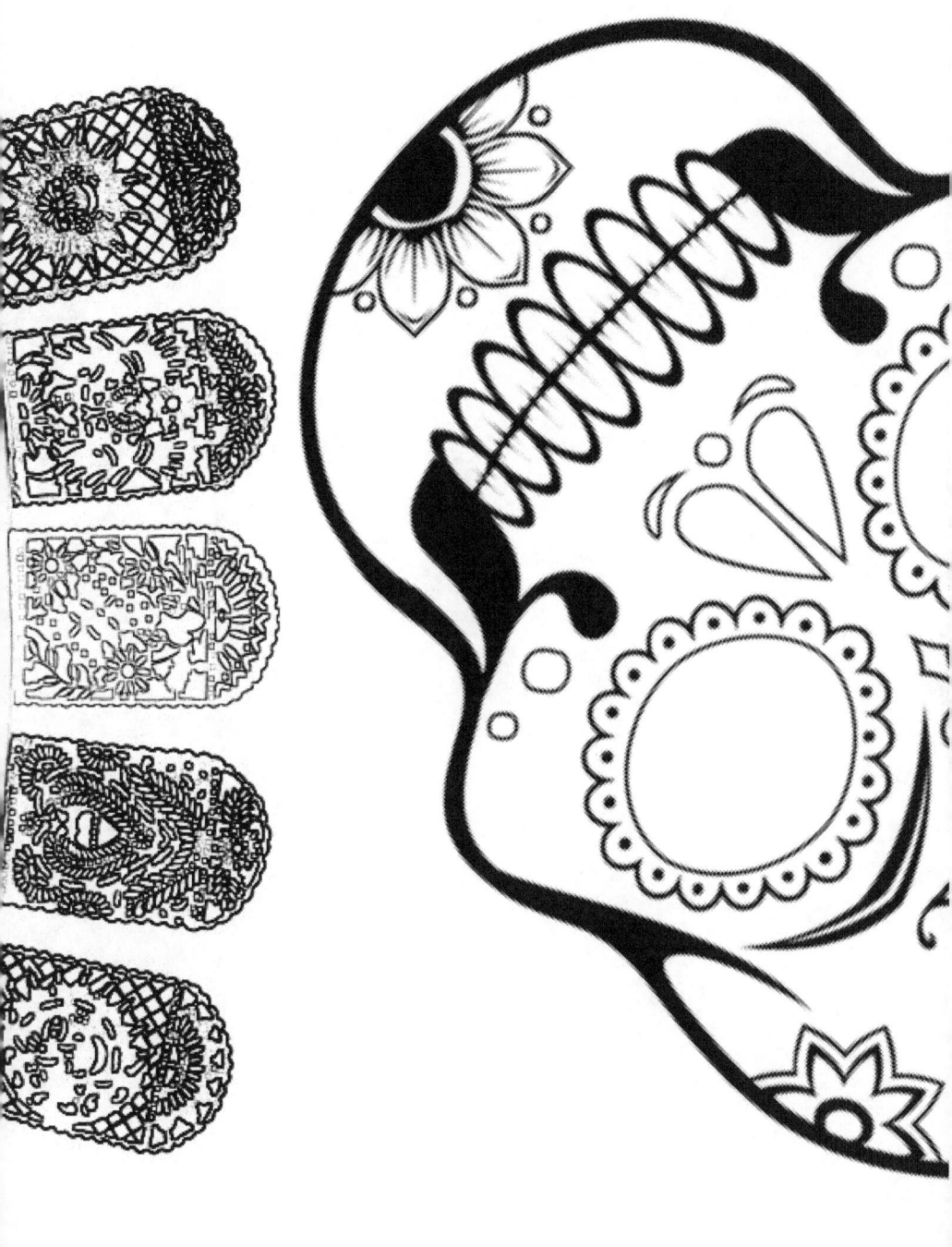

www.ingramcontent.com/pod-product-compliance
Lightning Source LLC
Chambersburg PA
CBHW061157180526
45170CB00002B/845